Family Favorites

From an All-American Family of Lebanese Descent

"Sahtayn"

Joyce Brown

Joyce Brown

LifeRich Publishing is a registered trademark of The Reader's Digest Association, Inc.

LifeRich Publishing books may be ordered through booksellers or by contacting:

LifeRich Publishing
1663 Liberty Drive
Bloomington, IN 47403
www.liferichpublishing.com
1 (888) 238-8637

ISBN: 978-1-4897-1328-5 (sc)
ISBN: 978-1-4897-1329-2 (hc)
ISBN: 978-1-4897-1327-8 (e)

Library of Congress Control Number: 2017950058

Print information available on the last page.

LifeRich Publishing rev. date: 8/9/2017

This book was written in honor of my mother.

Mom and Dad on December 2, 1944, when it all started.

Contents

Pocket Bread and Things Made with Pocket Bread — 94

Casseroles, Soups, and Stews — 101

Desserts — 121

Preface

Our mother was a holy and devout Catholic and wonderful cook. We encouraged Mom to write a cookbook years ago. She put all our favorite Lebanese and American dishes into print. The problem is that if you didn't make the dish with her, you cannot figure it out from her book because there isn't enough detail. Oftentimes, family members, mostly of the younger generations, call me for directions. After I retired from federal service, I decided to test every recipe and rewrite Mom's book with detailed directions and photos. Mom is in heaven now, but I know she would love that I am continuing the Lebanese and American traditions while adding a few of my own. I mention American because there are also wonderful American family recipes in every chapter.

All four of my grandparents were born in Lebanon and migrated to the United States. My mother was born at Providence Hospital in Seattle and raised in Bellevue, Washington. My father was born at home in Manchester, New Hampshire. They met when Dad was stationed at Fort Lewis. They were married on December 2, 1944.

I grew up the middle child of nine children in Bellevue, Washington. I learned to cook at a very young age, and I liked helping in the kitchen. Growing up, we ate mainly Lebanese food, which is popularly labeled these days as Mediterranean food. All eight of my siblings like to cook, and each one has a specialty. Each has contributed to this collection of family favorites.

When I was in seventh grade, everyone in the class was supposed bring a baby picture into school. Sister Carmel Joseph, our teacher, posted them so we could see who could identify the most classmates. Being the fifth child, this was the only baby picture of me that existed. It was really hard for my classmates to guess this one.

I'm not sure the exact date, but the year is 1954. From left are
Larry, Dad, me, Janice, Michael, Mom, and Chuck.

My brother Michael is one year older than I am. When we were in grade school, all nine siblings were living at home. We had two refrigerators, one for food and one for milk. Those were still the days when milkmen delivered milk. Our milkman was Rudy. He was cool. Sometimes, he would watch cartoons with us. Mom even had him take out the garbage a time or two. It didn't bother him. Once in a while, he would leave a gallon of chocolate milk. That was an ultimate treat. Rudy came three times a week and filled one refrigerator with milk. One day, just after Rudy had delivered the milk, Michael brought a friend home. His friend's name was Richard, and he was an only child. Michael opened the refrigerator to get milk, and Richard exclaimed, "Wow! My mom only buys a quart a week!"

Mom was sitting at the desk. She laughed and said, "We spill that much at one meal." No kidding we did!

When Mom went to the grocery store, she took one of us with her because she always needed two carts. Sometimes, two of us would go because she needed three carts. When Mom would spend more than $100 at the grocery store, the manager would give her a gallon of ice cream for free. Can you imagine any store doing that today? I remember coming home from the grocery store one day and helping to put things away. It was time to start dinner, and Mom was exhausted. She took the hamburger out of the package, put it on a baking pan, and started to put it in the oven. I took the hamburger and made her sit down. With her direction, I made a meatloaf, vegetables, potatoes, and a salad. My first complete meal at age eight. It amazes me when I think about all the meals Mom put on the table. Dinner was at six sharp. We always ate dinner together. After the carnage, we would talk and laugh. My oldest brother, Chuck, would always stuff his napkin in the bottom of his glass. Mom would always scold him, and the younger sisters always laughed at him. Wonderful memories.

Back row, standing, from left: Janice, Uncle Toofy, George, me, Mike, Mary Ann, Sally, and Chuck.
Front row, sitting, from left: Larry, Aunt Inez, Dad, Jamilie, and Uncle John.

Here we all are on November 20, 2016, Dad's ninety-eighth birthday. My mom's two brothers and our aunt are with us. Not only am I blessed with so many loving siblings, their spouses, and their families, but I also have a fine son and his beautiful wife. Their two oldest boys are in high school, and their daughter is in grade school. If it weren't for the boys, I would not have been able to navigate through the computer work. Twenty-five years ago, I married a mountain man from Idaho, Joe. We met when we were both working for the Department of Defense. We are both retired now, and life is great. Joe already had a son when we met. Several years back, he married an Idaho girl, and they had a son, a cute little guy. He will be going into kindergarten in the fall. Joe's son also has another son who is twenty-one and on his own.

Acknowledgments

I want to thank all my brothers and sisters as well as their spouses for the wonderful recipes they contributed. I also want to thank my sister Janice for all her help with the writing.

Introduction

This book is a collection of family-pleasing, Lebanese recipes. Until recently, our recipes were handed down by daughter watching mother. This method seems no longer practical, so I am writing these recipes for my family and friends. My way might be the same as others do things, or it might be quite different. We all need to find the ways that work for us.

There is something in Lebanese cooking for everyone: the gourmet, the dieter, the vegetarian, and the health food enthusiast. Broaden your culinary talent, prepare delicious and distinctive dishes, impress family and friends, and enjoy cooking and sharing a meal. Please enjoy, or as they say in Lebanon, "sahtayn", which means, "two healths to you."

Recipe Names

Lebanese titles? I know the Lebanese names for many these dishes, and there are others that I don't know. As for the proper way to pronounce and spell the Lebanese names, everyone pronounces and spells them differently. I have attempted to spell the recipe names phonetically.

Things to Keep on Hand

There are many items that can be kept in reserve. This is not an inclusive list.

Garlic-infused olive oil

Peel and mince six to eight garlic cloves, and place in an 8-ounce jar. Fill the remainder of the jar with olive oil. Stir and store in refrigerator. I use it in so many recipes, including dips, salads, and main dishes. Use it in any recipe calling for olive oil and garlic.

Pantry Staples
salt
black pepper
cinnamon
allspice
cumin
white pepper
granulated garlic
onion powder
dried parsley
dried oregano
dried basil
paprika
cayenne pepper

mushrooms
converted rice
jasmine rice
vermicelli
garbanzo beans (chickpeas)
kidney beans
elbow macaroni
egg noodles
cream soups
tomato sauce
diced tomatoes
olive oil
vegetable or canola oil

Fresh Foods
tomatoes
lemons
cucumbers
leaf lettuce
romaine lettuce
iceberg lettuce
green onions (scallions)
sweet white onions
dry yellow onions
red onions
plain yogurt
garlic
parsley
spinach
carrots
white potatoes
red potatoes
celery

Kitchen Tools

Heavy-duty mixer: A good stand mixer is a must. My mixer is very old. It has worked great even after falling five feet from a shelf, which I built, in the garage. That happened thirty years ago. I'm a cook, not a carpenter. There are all kinds of designer casings these days. Be sure you like what you get because it will last a long time. Mine certainly has, and I use it a lot. I remember that my brother George came by the house one day. When he walked in, I was using my mixer. He laughed and said, "Joe's outside with his power tools, and you're in here with your power tools."

Food processor: This tool makes many preparation jobs easy.

Baking dishes: All my baking dishes are the older tempered glass. They not as deep as the casserole dishes available today. If you have deeper dishes, you will not need to use as big a dish as stated in the recipe, though you may have to bake it a while longer. Oval dishes are very nice for casseroles as well.

Stovetop cookware: Always read the use-and-care guide for whatever type of cookware you purchase. The sizes in the recipes are what I have in my kitchen. If your stove-top cookware is slightly bigger or smaller, it will work. When cooking, be careful not to hit your utensils on the rims. It could dent the rim and ruin the seal. I recommend handwashing stainless steel cookware. Putting it in the dishwasher will eventually ruin the finish, which affects conductivity.

Nonstick and cast iron cookware: Check the use-and-care guide for washing instructions as well as oven temperature recommendations for both the pan and the lid. Never use spray oil or detergent on nonstick surfaces or cast iron, as both can damage the finish. Always be sure that cast iron is stored oiled and completely dry.

Enamel-coated cookware: Always read instructions for use and care as well as oven-use recommendations for the pans and lids. The main thing to remember with enamel is to not chip or scratch it. Be careful when washing.

Glass bowls: Be careful not to hit utensils on the rim. The glass could chip and end up in the food.

Breakfast

During the school year when we were growing up, Dad usually made breakfast. It was usually a couple of eggs and hot dogs fried—or should I say poached?—in olive oil. My dad loved hot dogs, so we had them most school day mornings. It isn't surprising that we all like hot dogs. They were served with pocket bread, tomato wedges, and milk.

A hint on cracking eggs: Always tap them lightly on a flat surface. Cracking an egg on the edge of a pan or bowl can cause shells to end up in the eggs.

Scrambled Lamb and Egg Omelet

Serves 6

We often had this for breakfast on Sunday after church. This is what we grew up knowing as an omelet. The first time I ordered an omelet in a restaurant, I thought it was so fancy—an individual serving folded in half. It was something we never saw at our house.

- *3 tablespoons olive oil*
- *1 pound leg of lamb, finely diced or coarsely ground*
- *1 medium sweet white or red onion, diced*
- *3 or 4 mint leaves, finely chopped*
- *12 eggs*
- *1/2 teaspoon salt*
- *1/4 teaspoon white pepper*
- *1/4 teaspoon ground allspice*
- *Lemon wedges and tomato wedges*

Heat the olive oil in a 10-inch skillet on medium-high heat. Add the lamb and onion and sauté until lamb is fully cooked. Add the mint to the lamb. Beat together the eggs and spices, and add to the cooked lamb and onions. Reduce heat to medium-low. Gently and constantly scrape bottom of pan with the spatula until they are set. Don't chop eggs; just scrape and turn. This way, there will be larger pieces of egg.

Serve with the lemon and tomato wedges. A squirt of lemon on the omelet is really good. Traditionally, all meals are served with pocket bread. When eating eggs and omelets, break a piece of bread and use it to pick up a bite. My dad called them boats, so we all—including my son and grandchildren—do the same. It's a tradition. My husband likes to stuff the omelet in the pocket bread. Of course, you can also use a fork.

Kibbi Omelet

Serves 4

- 1 tablespoon butter
- 1/2 pound coarsely ground lamb
- 1/4 cup pine nuts
- 1 medium dry yellow onion, finely chopped
- salt, pepper, and ground allspice to taste
- 8 eggs
- 1 cup plain yogurt or milk
- 4 or 5 mint leaves, minced
- 1/2 teaspoon salt
- 1/4 teaspoon pepper
- Dash ground allspice

Preheat oven to 375 degrees F. Melt the butter in a 10-inch ovenproof skillet over medium heat. Add the lamb, pine nuts, onion, salt, pepper, and allspice, and sauté until the lamb is cooked. Beat eggs with yogurt or milk; stir in mint, salt, pepper, and allspice; and pour into skillet. Bake 15 to 20 minutes or until set.

Zucchini Omelet

Serves 4

- 8 eggs
- 1 cup plain yogurt or milk
- 1/2 teaspoon salt
- 1/4 teaspoon pepper
- 2 tablespoons olive oil
- 1 tablespoon butter
- 2 cups zucchini, diced
- 1/2 medium sweet white onion or 3 green onions, chopped
- 4 ounces feta cheese, crumbled

Preheat oven to 375 degrees F. In a small bowl, beat eggs, yogurt or milk, salt, and pepper. Set aside.

Heat olive oil and butter in 10-inch ovenproofskillet on medium-high heat. Add zucchini and onions. Sauté until zucchini begins to brown. Stir in the egg mixture. Sprinkle feta over top. Bake 15–20 minutes or until set.

This can also be made with 3 cups of spinach or 2 cups of asparagus in place of zucchini. A combination of any two or three is good as well.

George's Spinach and Eggs

Serves 1

My brother George came up with this recipe.

- *1 cup fresh spinach*
- *1 green onion, chopped*
- *2 strips bacon, chopped*
- *2 eggs*
- *1 tomato, sliced or chopped*

Place spinach and green onion on a small plate. Arrange tomatoes on the side. In a 10-inch skillet, brown bacon on medium-high heat. When crisp, remove and sprinkle over top of spinach. Do not remove the grease. Reduce heat to medium-low, and in the same skillet, cook the eggs. They will pick up bits of the bacon that are left in the pan. Don't disturb the eggs until ready to remove from pan, and they will cook perfectly for sunny-side up.

Joe's Favorite Breakfast Wraps

Serves 8

My husband and I usually eat breakfast at different times. I need to eat soon after I get up. He can wait until 10 a.m. or later. Also, we don't eat the same thing for breakfast, so I like to make big batches of breakfast wraps. He really likes them. When I make these for my son and teenage grandsons, I don't need to freeze any. My daughter-in-law tells me they disappear quickly.

- 10 eggs
- 1 tablespoon hot sauce of choice
- 1 tablespoon seasoning salt of choice
- 1 pound country sausage
- 4 tablespoons canola oil, divided
- 2 cups shredded hash brown potatoes
- 1 1/2 cups shredded cheddar or jack cheese
- 3 green onions, chopped
- 2 mild green chilies, chopped
- 8 large tortillas

Break the eggs in a large bowl. Add the hot sauce and seasoning salt. Beat on a mixer's low speed until combined. Set aside. Put 2 tablespoons of canola oil in a 10-inch skillet on medium-high and heat until oil is just hot. Crumble sausage into skillet and cook completely. Drain. Return sausage to skillet with the remaining 2 tablespoons of canola oil. Add the egg mixture and cook on medium-low heat, stirring frequently. When eggs are cooked, add potatoes and heat through. Remove from heat and add cheese, green onions, and chilies. Mix together. Place 1 cup of filling in a line on a tortilla. Fold bottom over filling.

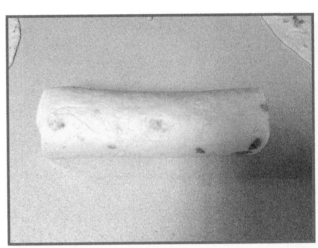

Fold sides of tortilla as shown and then finish rolling as you would a burrito.

Set the wraps on a tray and put them in the refrigerator to cool. When cool, put them into a zip-top food storage bag. I put two in my refrigerator and freeze the rest.

To heat, microwave 2 minutes for frozen or 1 minute for thawed. Then toast in a toaster oven for a crispy outside.

Sausage and Egg Muffins

Serves 6

- 1 pound country sausage
- 1 teaspoon butter
- 1/2 cup shredded Colby jack cheese
- 5 eggs
- 1/3 cup milk
- 1/2 teaspoon seasoning salt
- 1/4 teaspoon pepper
- 3 or 4 dashes hot sauce
- 6 English muffins

Preheat oven to 375 degrees F. Divide sausage into 6 equal portions. Form into patties, and place on a foil-lined baking sheet. Bake 20 minutes. Turn sausage. Bake 10 minutes longer. Remove from oven and place the sausage on paper towels to catch the grease. Meanwhile, butter a 4x6-inch baking dish. Spread the cheese in the bottom. In a medium bowl, beat the eggs, milk, salt, pepper, and hot sauce. Pour over cheese. Bake 40 minutes. Toast the English muffins. When everything is ready, cut the eggs into 6 equal portions. Assemble the sandwiches.

Linda's Blueberry Coffee Cake

Serves 12

This is a family favorite. My sister-in-law Linda gave me and everyone else in the family this recipe. She made this coffee cake, and Joe and I were lucky enough to get one.

For the Cake
- 1/2 cup Crisco, heaping
- 2 cups sugar
- 2 large eggs
- 1 cup buttermilk
- 1 teaspoon baking soda
- 1/4 teaspoon pure almond extract
- 1 teaspoon salt
- 3 1/2 cups all-purpose flour
- 3 cups of blueberries
- For the Topping
- 3/4 cup sugar
- 1/3 cup all-purpose flour
- 1/2 teaspoon cinnamon
- 1/3 cup butter, room temperature

For the Cake
Preheat oven to 400 degrees F. Cream together Crisco and sugar. Blend in 1 egg at a time. Slowly blend in buttermilk, soda, almond extract, salt, and flour. Fold in blueberries, and pour in one greased and floured 9x13-inch pan or two 8x8-inch pans. The batter will be thick.

For the Topping
In small bowl, combine sugar, flour, and cinnamon. Using fork or pastry knife, cut in butter until crumbly. Sprinkle over top of batter and bake 35–40 minutes or until a toothpick comes out clean. Do not touch the top for doneness. You will burn your finger.

Linda likes to use good, thick, rich, Bulgurian-style buttermilk. Dredge berries in 1/2 cup flour if you are using frozen berries and want to keep your batter nice and white. You can also use blackberries or chopped apples. This can also be baked in muffin tins. This cake freezes well and can be covered with foil and warmed in the oven.

Appetizers and Dips

Many Lebanese use pocket bread for the dips. My family also likes vegetables or pita chips with dips.

Mezza

Mezza is served in the Lebanese home before the meal or as food for an evening of visiting and sharing. Mezza consists mainly of Middle East olives called zaytun, cheeses, tomatoes, green onions, raw vegetables, and pocket bread. One may also serve hummus, labneh, and/or baba ganoush. You can also serve pickled vegetables and traditional pistachio nuts. Mezza is always served with pocket bread and a variety of appetizers. My sister Sally made all this. She is a fantastic cook, and her kitchen is amazing. Sally and her husband, Carl, are retired from the retail business.

Garbanzo Bean Dip–Hummus Bi Tahini

Makes 2 cups

- 2 (15.5-ounce) cans garbanzo beans or chickpeas, drained
- 1/2 cup tahini (sesame paste)
- 1/3 cup fresh lemon juice
- 1 clove garlic, mashed
- 1/4 teaspoon salt
- Dash cayenne pepper
- water
- 2–3 tablespoons olive oil
- fresh curly parsley or mint sprigs for garnish

Place first six ingredients in food processor or blender and blend well while adding water a tablespoon at a time until mixture reaches a smooth consistency. I like it a little thick.

Place in a shallow dipping bowl, and garnish with oil and parsley or mint.

Sally made this hummus. This is such a beautiful presentation.
Hummus is a wonderful complement to chicken, especially barbeque chicken.

Eggplant Dip–Baba Ganoush

Makes 2 cups

- 1 large eggplant
- 1/4 cup tahini (sesame paste)
- 1/4 cup fresh lemon juice
- 2 cloves garlic, minced
- 4-6 tablespoons olive oil, divided
- fresh curly parsley or greens for garnish

Cut eggplant in half lengthwise. Brush with 2-3 tablespoons olive oil. Grill 6–8 minutes on each side until tender, or leave eggplant whole (leave stem on) and pierce several times with a fork. Place on cookie sheet, and broil 6 minutes on each of the 4 sides. Remove from heat and cool. Peel the eggplant, and scrape the soft meat into a food processor. Blend with tahini, lemon juice, garlic, and remaining olive oil. Place in a shallow dipping bowl, and garnish with parsley or mint.

Yogurt Cheese Dip or Spread–Labneh

Makes 2 cups

My personal favorite! Labneh is made from laban, which is the Lebanese word for yogurt.

- 4 cups plain yogurt
- 2 garlic cloves, minced
- 2–3 tablespoons olive oil

Strain yogurt in a triple layer of cheesecloth or cheese strainer. Cover and set in refrigerator overnight or up to 2 days. When yogurt is firm, about the consistency of cream cheese, mix garlic and half the oil with strained yogurt. Place in a shallow dipping bowl, and drizzle with remaining oil. It is good on sandwiches too.

Sally's Zata

Serves 8

Zata is served as an appetizer. In our family, it is usually served as a part of Mezza.

- 1 Pocket Bread dough recipe
- 1/2 cup thyme seasoning, found in specialty stores, refer to photo
- 1/2 cup olive oil

When bread dough is ready, preheat oven to 375 degrees F.

Mix thyme seasoning with oil. Roll out bread dough, and place on oiled baking sheet. Spread oil and seasoning mix on dough.

Bake 15 minutes until brown and crispy.

MaryAnn's Shortcut Zata

- 1 package frozen bread dough rolls
- 1/2 cup thyme seasoning, found in specialty stores, refer to photo 25
- 1/2 cup olive oil

My sister, Mary Ann, made these. Mary Ann and her husband have a remodeling business, and she is always busy. This is her recipe, and she makes it frequently.

Place frozen rolls on oiled baking tray to thaw and rise according to package directions. When dough is finished rising, preheat the oven to 375 degrees F. Use a spoon to make an indent in the center of the roll. Mix seasoning and olive oil. Spoon seasoning into the center of each roll. Bake 15 minutes until brown and crispy. These are really good out of the oven or at room temperature.

Pocket Bread Chips (Better Known as Pita Chips)

Pita chips are easy to make and delicious with hummus, baba ganoush, and labni as well as many other appetizers and snacks.

- *6 loaves day-old pocket bread, cut into chip-sized pieces*
- *olive oil*
- *salt to taste*
- *white pepper to taste*
- *granulated garlic to taste*
- *onion powder to taste*
- *cumin to taste*

Preheat oven to 375 degrees F. Place bread in large bowl and drizzle with olive oil. Mix well and spread on ungreased cookie sheet. Sprinkle with salt, white pepper, granulated garlic, onion powder, and cumin to taste. Bake 15–18 minutes, stirring once. When they are golden brown and crispy, they are ready. Use for dips or in salads.

Makes a full 9-inch serving bowl as shown.

Raw Vegetables

Above is a beautiful vegetable tray that my sister Sally made for a wonderful Lebanese dinner. It is simple and appetizing.

Above is my vegetable tray.

Preparation

We all have certain vegetables that we like best. When I get home from the grocery store, I clean and prepare my vegetables for the week. I don't like buying precut raw vegetables. To me, they are dry and taste like preservatives. One thing that I learned is to keep vegetables moist for freshness and crispness. Here is what I normally do. I first wash everything.

Carrots and Celery

For the Carrots
Peel and cut into sticks, and place in a zip-top baggie. I save peelings for dog food.

For the Celery
Peel and cut into sticks, and place in a zip-top baggie. I like to peel the bitter strings off the celery and toss them.

Rinse once and then put just enough water in the baggie to cover the vegetables. Squeeze air out, and zip closed. Veggies will last a long time like this, and they will be ready to

snack on anytime. After a couple days, drain the water. The vegetables will still be good for several more days. Depending on how many vegetables you do at one time, you could pack the celery sticks in with the carrots.

Radishes

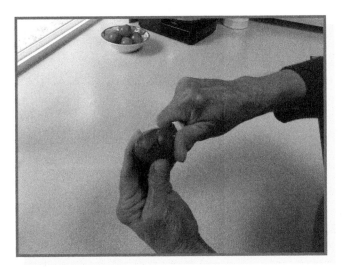

Cut greens and root off, and rinse again. I like to cut radish roses when I am doing a vegetable tray. To cut a radish rose, cut small slit half way down one side. Keep rotating and cutting slits around entire radish. Soak in water overnight in the refrigerator, and they open up beautifully.

If they are to go in a salad, I leave them whole until I make the salad. Whole radishes can just have a damp paper towel around them in a baggie. I save greens for dog food.

Cucumber

Peel strips lengthwise, leaving a strip of skin between peelings. Slice cucumber crossway for tray. Cucumber must be cut fresh the day it is used. When using for salad, I cut a piece off the cucumber peel and cut it. I then wrap the rest of the cucumber in a damp paper towel and wrap it in plastic. I save peelings and ends for dog food.

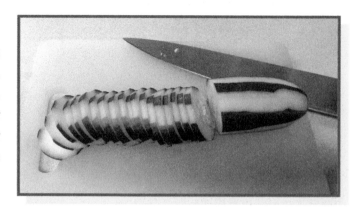

Broccoli and Cauliflower

These are best washed and cut fresh the day you use them. Cut into bite-sized florets whether you are putting them on a raw vegetable tray or cooking them. I save cores for dog food.

These are the vegetables I usually buy. There are many others to enjoy. If you noticed, I save all veggie scraps, except onions, for my dog food. Yes, I make dog food. Some of my brothers and sisters make fun of me. I don't care, though, because my dogs eat healthy food.

Pickled Vegetables

Some people like small jars, and some people like big jars. Originally, pickled vegetables were made to preserve in hot climates with little refrigeration. These were Mom's recipes. If you are into pickling, give them a try.

Pickled Eggplant

- 8 small, narrow Japanese eggplant
- 18 cloves garlic, minced
- 1 cup coarsely chopped nuts, such as pistachios or walnuts
- 2 tablespoons salt
- olive oil

Mix garlic and nuts, and set aside. Wash and peel eggplant, leaving stem. Parboil eggplant 1 minute. Slit eggplant lengthwise, and stuff with mixture of garlic and nuts. Place in sterilized jars, cover with olive oil, and seal. Let stand 5 weeks.

Pickled Turnips

- 2 medium beets
- 8 medium turnips
- 1 3/4 tablespoons salt
- 10 ounces vinegar
- 10 ounces water

Wash turnips and beets, cut into quarters, and pack in sterilized jars. Mix vinegar with water and salt. Fill jars with liquid, seal, and let stand 3 weeks.

Pickled White Onions

- 15–18 small white onions
- 1 3/4 cups white vinegar
- 2 teaspoons salt

Choose the smallest onions. Peel, rinse, and place in sterilized jars. Boil vinegar and salt, and pour over onions while hot. Seal jars, and let stand 10 days.

Pickled Cauliflower

- 2 heads cauliflower
- 1 3/4 tablespoons salt
- 10 ounces vinegar
- 10 ounces water

Wash cauliflower and cut into florets. Boil 4 minutes, and place in sterilized jars. Mix vinegar with water and salt. Cover cauliflower with liquid, seal, and let stand 3 weeks. This also works with shredded cabbage.

Sealing Jars

Place jars in a canning pot, cover with water, and bring to boil. Boil 20 minutes.

Salads

When we were growing up, salad was always a main part of our dinner. We always made Mediterranean-style dressing. When my sister married a boy from Montana, he asked her one night if he could have another kind of dressing. She said, "What other kind of dressing is there?" We all thought it was funny, because we always thought of other types of dressings as something you got in a restaurant. That is when we all realized that you can have blue cheese or Thousand Island at home. Of course, that was in the late 1960s. Bottled dressings weren't that good yet. There was one other dressing we would have. In some recipes, Mom would like to use ranch dressing because it has all the right herbs and spices. She used a package that you mix with mayonnaise and sour cream. I still use that to this day. My grandchildren love it with fresh vegetables.

Tabouli

Tabouli

Serves 6

Traditional tabouli is prepared with medium-ground cracked wheat. There are some modern variations, such as using couscous or quinoa to replace the bulgur. I have tried both, and they are good.

- *1/2 cup bulgur (cracked wheat), medium grind*
- *1/2 cup fresh lemon juice*
- *2 bunches green onions, finely chopped*
- *4 bunches fresh curly parsley, finely chopped*
- *5 or 6 fresh mint leaves, chopped*
- *1/2 cup canola oil*
- *1 teaspoon salt*
- *1/3 teaspoon allspice*
- *1/2 teaspoon pepper*
- *6 medium tomatoes, diced*
- *diced cucumber or raw peas, optional*

Place bulgur in large bowl, and cover with water. Let stand for 2 minutes and drain. Pour lemon juice on drained bulgur. Add green onions, parsley, mint, oil, and spices, and mix together. Gently fold in tomatoes. Tabouli is best marinated a few hours. It will stay good a few days.

Yogurt and Cucumber Salad

Serves 6

This is refreshing and cool in the summer.

- 2 cucumbers, peel, quarter and slice
- 1 clove garlic, minced
- 1 tsp. salt
- 5 fresh mint leaves, chopped
- 1 quart plain yogurt

Wash and prepare cucumbers (there is no need to peel English cucumbers). In a large bowl, mix garlic, salt, and mint. Mix in yogurt, and fold in cucumbers.

Mediterranean Salad

Serves 6

- 1 clove garlic, minced
- 3/4 teaspoon salt
- 4 fresh mint leaves, finely chopped
- 3 tablespoons olive oil
- 1 teaspoons fresh lemon juice
- 1 teaspoon white vinegar
- dash pepper
- 5 ripe tomatoes, cut in wedges
- 14 to 16 Kalamata or Greek olives
- 6 ounces feta cheese, crumbled or chunked
- 10 to 12 arugula leaves

In a medium bowl, mix garlic, salt, and mint. Add olive oil, lemon juice, vinegar, and pepper. Stir together. Add remaining ingredients, except arugula, and combine. Place in serving bowl. Garnish with arugula.

Stuffed Tomato Salad

Serves 6

- 6 large tomatoes
- 1 clove garlic, minced
- 4 fresh mint leaves, minced
- 1/2 teaspoon salt
- 2 tablespoon olive oil
- 1 teaspoon white vinegar
- 2 cucumbers, peeled and diced
- 1 (15.5-ounce) can kidney beans, rinsed and drained
- 3 green onions, finely chopped

Boil 3 quarts water. Cut center core from tomatoes. Immerse tomatoes in boiling water for about 20 seconds. Peel immediately. Cut top of tomato off, and hollow out the pulp and seeds. Discard seeds, chop pulp, and set aside.

In a large bowl, mix garlic, mint, and salt. Add oil and vinegar. Whisk well. Add tomato pulp and remaining ingredients to dressing and toss. Let stand 5 minutes, and toss again. Place mixture into hollow tomatoes, and arrange on a serving plate. Shrimp, tuna, and cheese may be added to stuffing.

Cucumber and Tomato Salad

Serves 6

- 3 large tomatoes, diced
- 2 medium cucumbers, peeled, quartered, and sliced
- 1/2 medium red or sweet white onion, peeled, halved, sliced, and separated
- 6 fresh mint leaves, finely chopped
- 3 tablespoons olive oil
- 1 teaspoon fresh lemon juice
- 1/2 teaspoon white vinegar
- 1 clove garlic, minced
- 3/4 teaspoon salt
- dash pepper

Place first four ingredients in salad bowl. Mix oil, lemon juice, vinegar, garlic, salt, and pepper in a small jar or bowl. Toss vegetables with dressing.

Wonderful Summer Salad

Serves 8

For Salad

- 1 head romaine
- 1 head green or red leaf lettuce
- 3 medium tomatoes, diced
- 1 cucumber, peeled, quartered, and sliced
- 1/2 sweet white onion, thinly sliced

For Summer Salad Dressing

- 1/4 cup olive or vegetable oil
- 2 tablespoons fresh mint, finely chopped
- 1 clove garlic, minced
- 1 tablespoon lemon juice
- 1 tablespoon. white vinegar
- dash Tabasco
- 1/2 teaspoon salt
- 1/4 teaspoon pepper

For the Salad

Cut lettuce into desired size. In a large bowl, combine all ingredients.

For Summer Salad Dressing

Whisk all ingredients together in a small bowl or jar.
Pour over dressing over salad and toss.

Prepared ahead and ready to toss for dinner.

To prepare ahead, place tomatoes, cucumber, and onion in a large salad bowl and pour dressing over top. This allows the tomatoes, cucumber, and onion to marinate. Cut lettuce to desired size and place on top as shown. Cover and refrigerate until you are ready to serve. Then simply toss the salad.

Fattoush

Serves 6

- 2 cups pita chips or toasted day-old pocket bread cut into small squares
- 6 leaves romaine or green leaf lettuce, washed and cut into 1-inch pieces
- 1 English cucumber, diced
- 2 medium tomatoes, diced
- 1/2 cup red onion, halved and sliced thin
- 1/2 cup fresh curly parsley, finely chopped
- 1/4 cup fresh mint, finely chopped

For the Dressing

- 1/4 cup olive oil
- 1/8 cup fresh lemon juice
- 1 clove garlic, minced
- 1/2 teaspoon salt
- 1/2 teaspoon freshly ground pepper

For the Fattoush

In a large salad bowl, combine chips, prepared vegetables, and herbs.

For the Dressing

Mix all ingredients in a small bowl or jar. Combine.

Pour dressing over salad and toss.

Make-Ahead Vegetable Salad

Serves 8

- One head green leaf lettuce
- 1/2 English cucumber
- 3 green onions
- 3 radishes
- 1 carrot

Cut lettuce into desired size. Quarter and slice cucumber. When using an English cucumber, there is no need to peel. Slice the green onions and radishes. Shave carrot with a peeler or grate. Layer as pictured.

When I make salad, I make a big bowl. I don't always use the same vegetables. I like to change it up. To keep salad fresh, I put a paper towel over it and sprinkle with water until the towel is just damp. I seal the top and put it in the refrigerator. It lasts a long time that way. The secret to making vegetables last is keeping them moist. I put dressing on when we eat.

Traditional Coleslaw

Serves 16

- 1 head green cabbage, shredded
- 1 head red cabbage, shredded
- 1 sweet white onion, shredded
- 2 tablespoons mustard seed
- 2 tablespoons sweet relish
- 1 tablespoon Worcestershire sauce
- 1 tablespoon apple cider vinegar
- 1/2 cup vegetable or canola oil

Put cabbage and onion in a large mixing bowl. In a small bowl or jar, mix remainder of ingredients. Pour over cabbage and toss. Cover and refrigerate. This slaw will last several days. This recipe makes a large amount and can easily be halved.

My Own Coleslaw

Serves 16

- *1 head green cabbage, shredded*
- *1 head red cabbage, shredded*
- *1 carrot, shredded*
- *1/2 cup chopped fresh curly parsley*
- *1/2 cup mayonnaise*
- *2 tablespoons apple cider vinegar*
- *2 tablespoons sugar*
- *1 tablespoons celery salt*

Put cabbage, carrot, and parsley in a large mixing bowl. In a small bowl, mix remainder of ingredients. Pour over cabbage and toss. Cover and refrigerate. This slaw will last several days. This recipe makes a large amount and can easily be halved.

Pineapple Coleslaw

Served 6

- *1/2 head green cabbage, washed and shredded*
- *8-ounce can pineapple tidbits, drained, juice reserved*
- *1/2 cup white raisins*
- *1/4 cup dates, chopped*
- *1/4 cup fresh cilantro, chopped*
- *1/4 cup mayonnaise*
- *2 tablespoons reserved pineapple juice*
- *Shredded cabbage.*

Put cabbage, pineapple, raisins, dates, and cilantro in a large bowl. In a small bowl, mix mayonnaise and pineapple juice. Toss all ingredients together. This will last 2–3 days. Sometimes, I put chopped apple on top of the slaw when serving.

Potato Salad

You must try this recipe. It is really good.

For the Dressing
- 1/2 cup vegetable or canola oil
- 2 tablespoons white vinegar
- 2 tablespoons sweet pickle juice
- 2 tablespoons dried parsley flakes
- 1 teaspoon salt
- 1 teaspoon celery salt
- 1 teaspoon paprika
- 1/2 teaspoon granulated garlic

For the Salad
- 6 medium potatoes, about 2 1/2 pounds
- 3 teaspoons salt, divided
- 4 hardboiled eggs
- 6 slices cucumber chips, chopped
- 8 black olives, sliced
- 3 sweet pickles, sliced
- 1/2 medium sweet white onion, diced
- 1/2 cup celery, diced
- 3/4 cup mayonnaise, divided

For the Dressing
Whisk all ingredients together and set aside.

For the Salad
Cook the potatoes and eggs. For the potatoes, wash and cut in half. Place in a large saucepan, and cover with water. Add 2 teaspoons salt, and bring to boil. Cover and reduce heat to medium low. Boil potatoes until tender, approximately 25 minutes depending on the size of the potatoes. When fork tender, drain water and let potatoes cool until you can handle them. Peel potatoes and refrigerate until cold.

For the eggs, place in a small saucepan and cover with water. Add 1 teaspoon salt and bring to boil. When water begins to boil, turn heat to medium low, cover, and cook for 9 minutes. Remove from heat and run cold water over eggs until cool. Peel and refrigerate until cold.

Prepare cucumber chips, olives, pickles, onion, and celery, and set aside. When potatoes and eggs are cold, dice and place in a large mixing bowl. Add cucumber chips, olives, pickles, onion, and celery to potatoes. Pour dressing over top and add 1/4 cup mayonnaise. Gently toss and allow a few hours for flavors to meld. When ready to serve, add 1/2 cup mayonnaise. Toss gently and put in a serving bowl. Like most potato salad, this is just as good the next day.

Blue Cheese Red Potato Salad– A Potluck Favorite

Serves 10–12

- 2 1/2 pounds red potatoes, washed and cut into 1-inch cubes
- 1 teaspoon salt
- 6 green onions, julienned
- 1/4 cup fresh curly parsley, chopped
- 8-ounce can sliced water chestnuts, cut in half
- 1/2–3/4 cup blue cheese dressing

In a medium saucepan, cover cut potatoes with water. Add salt. Bring to boil, cover, and reduce heat to medium low, and simmer 6 minutes or until potatoes are tender. Drain and place in large mixing bowl. Wash and prepare remaining vegetables while potatoes are cooling. Cool potatoes completely. Add remaining ingredients. Toss gently.

Spinach Salad

Serves 6

- 2 bunches fresh spinach, washed and cut into 1-inch pieces
- 4 green onions, finely chopped
- 1 bunch fresh curly parsley, finely chopped
- 1/4 cup vegetable or canola oil
- 4 tablespoons fresh lemon juice
- salt and pepper to taste

Wash and prepare all the vegetables. In a large bowl, toss all ingredients together. To make it even better, add 1 cup salad shrimp.

Pea Salad

Makes 4–5 cups

- 2 cups fresh or frozen peas
- 2 hardboiled eggs, chopped
- 4 green onions, chopped
- 4 slices crispy bacon, crumbled
- 1/2 cup sharp cheddar cheese, diced in pea-sized pieces
- 1/4 cup ranch dressing

Mix all ingredients for a delicious salad. To make it even better, add 1 cup salad shrimp or tuna.

Tuna with Peas

Serves 6

- *12 ounces fresh or frozen peas, thawed*
- *12-ounce can white tuna, drained and flaked*
- *1/2 cup mayonnaise*
- *4 green onions, sliced*
- *1 tablespoon lemon juice*
- *1/2 teaspoon curry powder*
- *1 head romaine or red leaf lettuce*

Mix all ingredients except lettuce. Break 6 leaves off the lettuce and place one on each of 6 salad plates. Shred the remaining lettuce and put a bed of lettuce on each plate. Serve 2/3 cup salad on each plate. Pretty and delicious.

Macaroni and Things Salad

Serves 10–12

- 1 1/2 cups salad macaroni
- 15.2-ounce can whole kernel corn, drained
- 1 cup mayonnaise or ranch dressing (for extra flavor)
- 4 ounces Colby cheese, grated
- 1/2 cup cucumber chips, diced
- 1/2 cup celery, diced
- 1/2 teaspoon granulated garlic
- dash curry powder

Cook macaroni according to package. Drain, rinse with cold water, drain well, and let cool. When cool, mix all ingredients together in a large bowl. Also delicious with shrimp, tuna, or chicken.

Yogurt and Macaroni Salad

Serves 6

- 2 cups cooked elbow macaroni, rinsed
- 1 clove garlic, minced
- 1 teaspoon salt
- 5 fresh mint leaves
- 1 cup plain yogurt or ranch dressing

Cook macaroni according to package directions. Allow macaroni to cool completely. In a medium bowl, mash garlic, salt and mint. Stir in yogurt and macaroni.

Mandarin Orange Couscous Salad

Serves 4

- 11-ounce can mandarin oranges
- 1 cup couscous
- 1 tablespoon butter
- 3 tablespoons canola oil
- 1/2 cucumber, peeled, quartered and sliced
- 3 green onions, sliced
- 1/2 sweet red pepper, diced

Drain oranges, reserving juice. Add water to orange juice to make 1 1/4 cup liquid. In a small saucepan, melt butter and brown couscous. When browned, pour liquid over couscous. Reduce heat to low. Cook 12 minutes, stirring frequently. Remove from heat, add oil and cool completely. Place in large bowl. Add remaining ingredients, and toss gently. Chill and serve.

Fancy Chicken Salad

Serves 6

This is elegant and delicious. It's a must-try salad.

- 2 half chicken breasts
- 1 1/2 teaspoons seasoning salt, divided
- 1/2 cup celery, diced
- 8-ounce can pineapple tidbits, drained
- 1/4 cup mayonnaise
- 3/4 cup sliced almonds
- 1 cup medium cheddar cheese cubes
- 1/2 cup provolone cheese cubes
- 2 teaspoons onion powder
- 2 teaspoons lemon juice
- 1/2 teaspoon salt
- 1/4 teaspoon white pepper
- 12 romaine or leaf lettuce leaves or 6 cups spinach greens

Place chicken in a small saucepan. Sprinkle 1 teaspoon seasoning salt over top, cover with water, and bring to boil. Reduce heat to low, cover, and simmer 20 minutes. When cooked, remove from broth and chill in refrigerator. Cut chicken into cubes. While chicken is chilling, prepare the remaining ingredients. In a large bowl, mix remaining ingredients together except lettuce or spinach. Serve on lettuce leaves or a bed of spinach. Even better, warm it up, and have it in pocket bread or a croissant with a piece of leaf lettuce. Excellent!

Chicken Salad

Serves 6

- 2 cooked chicken breasts, cubed
- 1/2 cup celery, diced
- 1/4 cup mayonnaise
- 2 teaspoons dill weed
- 1 teaspoon onion powder
- 1 teaspoon granulated garlic
- 1/2 teaspoon salt
- 1/2 teaspoon seasoning salt
- 1/4 teaspoon white pepper

In a large bowl, mix all ingredients together. Great in pocket bread over a bed of lettuce or stuffed in a tomato. It is particularly good on a croissant with a little red onion and a piece of leaf lettuce.

Jell-O, the Forgotten Fun Food

When we were growing up, Jell-O was very popular. There are so many fun ways to make delicious Jell-O. It is a budget stretcher and a good way to get children to eat fruit in the winter.

Frosted Lemon Jell-O

Serves 12

This Jell-O is a family tradition at our holiday meals. It is sweet and a little savory. Everyone loves it. I always make this the day before serving it. I have a special apple-shaped bowl that I always use. It holds one recipe perfectly. A glass 9x13-inch dish can be easily used as well. With my large family, I always need to double the recipe (as pictured here). The topping also makes a great fruit salad dressing or fruit dip.

For the Jell-O

- 6-ounce box lemon Jell-O
- 2 cups boiling water
- 2 cups cold water
- 20-ounce can crushed pineapple, drained (reserve juice)
- 2 sliced bananas
- 1 cup mini marshmallows

For the Topping

- 1 cup reserved pineapple juice
- 1/2 cup sugar
- 3 tablespoons all-purpose flour
- Dash salt
- 1 egg
- 2 tablespoons butter
- 1 cup heavy cream
- 3 tablespoons Parmesan cheese
- 1/2 cup finely grated medium cheddar cheese

Frosted Lemon Jell-O

For the Jell-O

In a large glass bowl, dissolve Jell-O in boiling water and whisk for full two minutes until Jell-O is thoroughly dissolved. Add cold water. Layer pineapple, bananas, and marshmallows in a glass serving dish. Carefully pour Jell-O into dish. Chill until firm.

For the Topping

Combine pineapple juice, sugar, flour, salt, and egg in small saucepan. Whisk until smooth, and cook on medium heat, stirring constantly. When mixture becomes thick, remove from heat. Add butter. Stir until butter is incorporated. Pour into a bowl, and place a thin layer of plastic wrap over surface. Allow to cool to room temperature, and refrigerate until chilled. When chilled, whip the heavy cream to stiff peaks. Gently fold pineapple curd into whipped cream and frost the Jell-O. Sprinkle the cheeses over the top and then chill a couple hours to set topping.

Fancy Lime Jell-O

Serves 6

- 🍴 *6-ounce box lime Jell-O*
- 🍴 *20-ounce can crushed pineapple with juice*
- 🍴 *2 cups small-curd cottage cheese*

Prepare Jell-O according to package directions but with one less cup cold water. Allow Jell-O to cool 10 minutes. Place pineapple and cottage cheese in a glass bowl. Gently pour Jell-O over top. Refrigerate until set.

Lime Jell-O with Mint Pears

Serves 6

- 🍴 *6-ounce box lime Jell-O*
- 🍴 *15.5-ounce can mint pears, drained and sliced*

Prepare Jell-O according to package directions. Allow Jell-O to cool 10 minutes. Place pears in a glass bowl. Gently pour Jell-O over top. Refrigerate until set.

Mandarin Orange Jell-O

Serves 6

- 2 cups boiling water
- 3-ounce box orange Jell-O
- 1/4-ounce package plain gelatin
- 11-ounce can mandarin oranges
- 2 bananas
- 2 cups mini marshmallows

In two cups boiling water, mix Jell-O and gelatin for two minutes in a 3-cup measuring cup. Add juice from mandarin oranges and ice to make three cups total. Stir until ice melts. In a serving bowl, place mandarin oranges and sliced bananas. Pour Jell-O over fruit. Sprinkle marshmallows over top, allowing them to float. Refrigerate until set.

Strawberry Shortcake Jell-O

For the Jell-O

- 6-ounce box strawberry Jell-O
- 3 cups angel food cake cubes
- 3 cups strawberries, sliced

For the Whipped Topping

- 1 1/2 cups heavy cream
- 1/4 cup powdered sugar
- 1 teaspoon vanilla extract

For the Jell-O

Prepare Jell-O according to package instructions. In a serving bowl, layer cake and strawberries. Pour Jell-O over top. Refrigerate until set.

For the Whipped Topping

In a chilled bowl, whip all ingredients until stiff peaks form.

Cover set Jell-O with whipped topping. Allow to set in refrigerator 1 hour.

Vegetables, Rice, and Couscous

Zahlia

Janice's Fresh Garden Stew–Zahlia

Serves 12

From my sister Janice, a retired teacher and great cook

- *28-ounce can tomato sauce*
- *5 quarts water*
- *1 medium dry yellow onion, thinly sliced*
- *3 garden tomatoes, diced*
- *3 small zucchini, sliced in thick chunks*
- *18 fresh green beans, whole*
- *1/3 orange pepper, diced*
- *1 small white potato, diced*
- *1 red potato, diced*
- *3 cloves garlic, minced*
- *1 tablespoon salt*
- *1 teaspoon pepper*
- *4 sprigs fresh curly parsley, stems removed and minced*

Put all ingredients in a 12-quart pot. Bring to a boil, cover, reduce heat to medium low, and simmer 45 minutes. This stew is good warm or cold. Great for a crowd.

Jamilie's Ullie Green Beans, Lebanese-style

Serves 6

"Ullie" refers to the method of cooking. We enjoyed these often growing up. This recipe is from my sister Jamilie. She is a nurse and very healthy. She makes the best vegetable dishes.

- 1 sweet onion, thinly sliced
- 2 tablespoons extra-virgin olive oil, divided
- 10 cloves garlic, peeled
- 1–1 1/2 pounds fresh green beans, ends removed and snapped in half
- 1/2 teaspoon salt

In a 10-inch skillet, add 1 tablespoon olive oil on medium-high heat. sauté onions and garlic until slightly brown and caramelized, about 6 minutes. Remove from heat and set aside. In a large pot, add beans and remaining olive oil. Sauté beans until brown, about 6 minutes.

Combine onions with beans, and season with salt. Cover, reduce heat to low, and simmer 25 minutes.

This is Jamilie making her wonderful ullie beans.

Cold Vegetable Medley–Umsuhah

Serves 12

In the summer, Mom used to take us to the lake to picnic and swim all day. I remember this was one of the things that she would bring to eat. We all enjoyed eating vegetables.

- 3 tablespoons canola oil
- 1 small eggplant, peeled and cut in 2-inch pieces
- 2 zucchini, sliced into 2-inch wheels
- 1 sweet white onion, thinly sliced
- 4 cloves garlic, smashed with the side of knife and sliced in half
- 2 teaspoons salt
- 2 teaspoons pepper
- 15.5-ounce can garbanzo beans, drained
- 15.5-ounce can diced tomatoes with juice

Preheat oven to 425 degrees F. Pour oil into a 9x13-inch baking dish. Layer eggplant, zucchini, onion, and garlic into baking dish. Toss to coat vegetables with oil. Add salt and pepper. Bake uncovered for 10 minutes. Remove from oven, and reduce heat to 300 degrees F. Add beans and tomatoes to the baking dish. Cover with foil. Bake for an additional 45 minutes. Remove from oven, uncover, and allow to cool. Serve cold with pocket bread.

Oven-Roasted Vegetables

Wash and cut vegetables to desired size. Place on an oven tray and drizzle with olive oil. Sprinkle with salt and pepper. Roast in oven uncovered at 400 degrees F for 15–20 minutes or until brown.

Asparagus

Broccoli

Any vegetable is good for roasting. Be creative. I roast a variety of colorful vegetables together. I like to put garlic cloves in my roasted vegetables. They really add flavor.

Mixed Vegetables

Wash and cut vegetables to desired size. When cutting mixed vegetables for roasting, they should be uniform in size. This allows the vegetables to cook evenly. Place in a flat baking dish. Drizzle with olive oil. Sprinkle with salt and pepper. Roast uncovered at 400 degrees F for 15–20 minutes until brown.

Carrots

Slice desired amount of carrots. Pictured are two carrots. Place them in a baking dish with 2 teaspoons melted butter and 2 teaspoons brown sugar. Mix and bake at 375 degrees for 30 minutes. Do the same thing in a skillet with some thinly sliced onions and caramelize them. That is also very good.

Red Potatoes

Wash and cut in half. Place in baking pan, coat with melted butter, sprinkle with salt, and roast uncovered at 400 degrees F for 15–20 minutes or until brown.

Fresh Yams

Fresh yams are always good. I like to wash them, wrap them in foil, and bake at 400 degrees F for 45–50 minutes until tender. When they come out, the peel comes off very easily with a fork. I cut them into chunks, and we eat them with butter, salt, and pepper. So good any time of year. The dogs like yams in their food as well.

Stove-Top Vegetables

Wash and cut vegetables to desired size. Using a skillet, heat 2 tablespoons olive oil and 1 tablespoons butter on medium-high heat. Sauté vegetables until brown. Again, be creative. Any vegetable is good sautéed. Try eggplant, cauliflower, onion, green beans, red, or white potatoes.

Zucchini

Mashed Potatoes

Wash and peel potatoes. Cut into chunks, place in pot, and cover with water. Salt the water as desired. Bring to boil. Reduce heat to low, cover potatoes, and cook 20–25 minutes until tender. Drain. Add 1 tablespoon butter for every two potatoes. Splash in some milk but not too much. Mash by hand. Sometimes, I put a couple cloves of garlic in with the potatoes. They add a wonderful flavor. Some people in the family put cream cheese in their mashed potatoes too.

Fresh Beets

Serves 4

- 4 *fresh beets, washed twice*
- 1 *tablespoon apple cider vinegar*
- 1 *tablespoon sugar*
- 1 *tablespoon water*

Cut greens from beets. Peel beets. Chop greens in large pieces. Cut beets in half and slice. Place beets, greens, apple cider vinegar, sugar, and water in a saucepan. Bring to boil, reduce heat to low, and simmer 10 minutes. Beets are easy and delicious prepared this way. Try Swiss chard prepared this way. Mom made it a lot.

Sweet and Tart Cabbage

Serves 2

- 1 tablespoon butter
- 1 tablespoon lemon juice
- 1 teaspoon sugar
- 1/2 teaspoon celery salt
- 2 cups shredded cabbage

Pictured here is 2 cups of shredded cabbage. When finished cooking, there will be about 1 cup cabbage, which is a perfect side dish for two.

In a 2-quart saucepan, melt butter over medium-high heat. Add lemon juice, sugar, and celery salt. Add cabbage. Cook down until cabbage browns. It is a sweet-tart vegetable dish that everyone will enjoy. For a less sweet flavor, use 2 teaspoons apple cider vinegar instead of the lemon juice and only 1/4 teaspoon celery salt.

Grilled Vegetables

Summer is a great time for grilling. I like to cook my vegetables on the barbeque. That is absolutely the best way to cook them. The flavor from the grill is wonderful. Be sure to always wash vegetables before cooking.

Interesting fact about foil: Joe and I used to watch a show called *How It's Made*. One episode showed how foil was made. It comes off a huge roller and has one shiny side and one dull side. When asked if it made a difference in cooking properties regarding which side of the foil is out, the foil guy said absolutely not. It cooks exactly the same on both sides.

Grilled chicken, potatoes, and asparagus with cut vegetables and hummus.

Potatoes

Scrub potatoes clean and slice. Butter a piece of foil. Place sliced potatoes on half of the buttered foil. Fold foil over potatoes and seal sides, leaving only the end open to release steam. Cook over hot coals for 10 minutes per side for crispy potatoes.

Asparagus

To grill asparagus, drizzle with olive oil, sprinkle with salt and pepper, and place directly on grate for 5–7 minutes. Sometimes I sprinkle an organic salt substitute on my vegetables. You can grill zucchini the same way. Just cut it in half lengthwise, and grill cut-side down. Try grilling an ear of corn that way too. So good!

Grilled Onions and Garlic

Grilled rib steak with grilled onion and garlic alongside with golden potatoes and pineapple coleslaw.

Peel 10 garlic cloves, and cut each in half. Peel and slice a large sweet white onion. Place vegetables on foil, drizzle with melted butter, and close foil packet. Place on grill. Start onions and garlic with steaks, and it will all be ready at the same time.

Grill-Roasted Vegetables

Put vegetables in a foil pan, and drizzle with canola oil, salt, and pepper. Roast them on the grill. Any vegetable that can be roasted in the oven can be cooked on the grill. I buy foil pans cheap at the local dollar store.

Steamed Rice

Makes 6 cups

Baked chicken with steamed rice, hummus, and salad.

- 2 cups uncooked white rice (converted rice works well in Lebanese cooking)
- 2 tablespoons butter
- 3 3/4 cups hot water or chicken broth
- 1/2 teaspoon salt

In a 2-quart saucepan, brown the rice in butter over medium heat. Browning the rice adds a great toasted flavor. When rice is golden, deglaze the pan by adding water or broth and salt. Be careful; it will steam. Reduce heat to low, cover, and cook 18–20 minutes.

Steamed Rice with Vermicelli

Makes 6 cups

Steamed Rice with Vermicelli, kibbi, and green salad with yogurt dressing.

- *1 3/4 cups uncooked white rice (converted rice works well in Lebanese cooking)*
- *4 ounces vermicelli noodles, broken into 1-inch pieces*
- *2 tablespoons butter*
- *4 cups water or chicken broth, hot*
- *1/2 teaspoon salt*

In a 2-quart saucepan, brown rice and vermicelli in melted butter over medium heat. Browning the rice and noodles adds great toasted flavor. When rice and vermicelli are golden, deglaze the pan by adding water or broth and salt. Be careful; it will steam. Reduce heat to low, cover, and cook 18–20 minutes.

Rice Dressing

Rice dressing is definitely a family favorite.
It is always on our Thanksgiving table, right
next to the bread dressing. I like cranberry
sauce on the rice dressing and gravy on bread
dressing. Of course, we have this other times
of the year too.

- *3 tablespoons butter, divided*
- *1/2 cup pine nuts*
- *1/2 cup sweet white onion, chopped*
- *1/2 cup celery, finely chopped*
- *2 cups uncooked white rice (converted rice works well in Lebanese cooking)*
- *4 ounces vermicelli noodles, broken into 1-inch pieces*
- *4 cups hot water or chicken broth*
- *1 teaspoon salt*
- *1/2 teaspoon pepper*
- *1/4 teaspoon cinnamon*

Melt 2 tablespoons butter in a 5-quart pot over medium-high heat. Brown pine nuts, and set aside. In the
same pot, sauté onions and celery until transparent. Set aside.

In the same pot, add remaining butter. Sauté rice and vermicelli until lightly brown. Return pine nuts, onion, and celery to pot.

Deglaze the pan by adding hot water or broth as well as the salt, pepper, and cinnamon. Be careful; it will steam. Cover, reduce heat to low, and simmer 20 minutes.

Couscous

Makes 3 cups

This is delicious and versatile pasta. You can use it in place of rice as a side dish, or it can be used in salads and soups.

- *2 tablespoons butter*
- *1 cup couscous*
- *1 1/4 cups hot water or chicken broth*

In a 2-quart saucepan, melt butter over medium heat, and add the couscous. Brown couscous, stirring frequently at first. When it begins to brown, do not leave it. Stir constantly until golden brown. When golden, add hot water or chicken broth. Be careful; it will steam. Cook uncovered 10–12 minutes, stirring occasionally. Couscous should be tender.

Lebanese Main Dishes

Tips

- Regular or medium-ground meat can be easily substituted in recipes that call for coarse-ground meat. Coarse ground is traditional, but most grocery stores only have medium ground meat. I usually grind my own.
- Kusa, grape leaves, and rolled cabbage can be made without the shoulder cuts, riblets, or chops.
- Many recipes call for pine nuts. They are good, but they are expensive. I buy them when I see them on sale. They can be optional in any recipe.
- Beef can usually be substituted for lamb
- Plain yogurt is used as a condiment for many dishes, much like sour cream.

Tips for Good Kibbi

Kibbi is a well-known Lebanese dish. The word "kubaybah" means to form a ball. Basically, the form for serving kibbi is in a ball or sphere with one exception. This is when it is baked flat in a pan.

Hints for kibbi:
- Ground leg of lamb is traditional, but lean ground beef is delicious as well.
- The two main ingredients in kibbi are ground meat and medium-ground bulgur. The ratio of meat to bulgur is:
  - 1 pound meat to 1 cup less 2 tablespoons bulgur for raw kibbi
  - 1 pound meat to 1 cup bulgur for cooked kibbi
- To make a dish gluten-free, quinoa can be substituted for bulgur.
- When patting kibbi flat for cooking, wet hands with a heavy saltwater solution (2 tablespoons salt to 1 cup water).
- When making raw kibbi, use only fresh leg of lamb, with all the fat and gristle cut away, that was ground the same day. Cook leftover raw kibbi the second day.
- If there is excess kibbi filling, it is great cooked and scrambled with eggs.
- Cooked kibbi may be frozen. When thawed, wrap in foil and reheat at 375 degrees F for 20 minutes.

Traditional Diamond Cut

Cutting kibbi or baklawa into a traditional diamond cut.

Cut lengthwise strips as shown. Next, cut diagonally as shown.

Raw Kibbi

Sally is pouring olive oil over the beautiful raw kibbi she made.
Mom always made the sign of the cross on raw kibbi. It is a Lebanese tradition.

- *1 3/4 cups medium-grind bulgur*
- *2 pounds fresh ground lamb, completely free of fat*
- *1 large sweet white onion, finely chopped or pulsed fine in food processor*
- *1 tablespoon salt*
- *1/2 teaspoon pepper*
- *5–6 mashed fresh mint leaves, if available*

In a large bowl, cover bulgur with cold water, soak 15 minutes, and drain. Add meat, onions, and spices to drained bulgur. Mix thoroughly while continuing to dip hands in cold water to make the mixture soft. Shape onto a platter garnished with onions, radishes, or other vegetables. Drizzle with olive oil. Cook any leftover the second day.

Basic Kibbi Filling–Hushwie

Makes 2 cups

- 1 tablespoon butter
- 1 pound coarsely ground lamb or beef
- 1/4 cup pine nuts
- 1 medium dry yellow onion, chopped
- 1/2 teaspoon salt
- 1/2 teaspoon pepper
- 1/4 teaspoon allspice

In a 10-inch skillet on medium heat, sauté all ingredients in butter until lamb is cooked. Allow to cool before filling kibbi.

Cooked Kibbi–Kibbi bis-Sayniyyi

Serves 10–12

This is very popular in the family, including in-laws and mountain men from Idaho.

- *2 cups medium-grind bulgur*
- *4 cups cold water*
- *2 pounds fresh lean ground lamb or beef (or 1 pound each)*
- *1 large sweet white onion, finely chopped or pulsed fine in food processor*
- *1 tablespoon salt*
- *1/2 teaspoon pepper*
- *1/4 teaspoon allspice*
- *1/4 cup olive oil*

In a large bowl, cover bulgur with 4 cups cold water, soak 15 minutes, and drain.

Add meat, onions, and spices to drained bulgur. Mix thoroughly. Pat into a lightly oiled 9x13-inch baking dish. For thinner kibbi, use a larger dish. If filling the kibbi, pat half the kibbi mixture into the baking dish, spread the basic kibbi filling over first layer, and pat remaining kibbi mixture over the top. Cut into traditional diamond cut (refer to photos of at beginning of chapter).

Pour 1/4 cup olive oil over kibbi. Bake at 375 degrees F for 35–40 minutes. Serve with salad, vegetables, and plain yogurt on the side.

Meatless Potato Kibbi—Kibbit Batata bis-Sayniyyi

Serves 6

- 1/2 cup medium-grind bulgur
- 1 1/2 cups mashed potato
- 1 cup mashed yams or pumpkin
- 1 small dry yellow onion, finely chopped or pulsed fine in food processor
- 1/4 cup all-purpose flour
- 2 teaspoons salt
- 1 teaspoon dried basil
- 1/2 teaspoon pepper
- 4 tablespoons canola or olive oil, divided

In a large bowl, cover bulgur with cold water, soak for 15 minutes, and drain. Add remaining ingredients, except oil, and mix well. Coat an 8x8-inch baking dish with 2 tablespoons oil. Pat kibbi mixture into baking dish. Cut into traditional diamond cut (refer to photos of at beginning of chapter). Pour remaining oil over top of kibbi. Bake at 375 degrees F for 35–40 minutes until golden brown.

Stuffed Kibbi Spheres—Erse

Serves 4

Erse, yogurt, tomato wedges, and roasted
vegetables.

- *1/2 cup bulgur, medium grind*
- *Half recipe Basic Kibbi Filling*
- *1 pound ground lamb*
- *1/2 sweet white onion, finely
  chopped*
- *1 teaspoon salt*
- *1/2 teaspoon pepper*
- *1/4 teaspoon allspice*

Divide Basic Kibbi Filling into 4 servings and set aside. In a large bowl, cover bulgur with cold water, soak
for 15 minutes, and drain. Add lamb, onions, and spices to drained bulgur and mix thoroughly.

Divide mixture into four even balls. Divide each ball in half. Pat half flat and form around bottom of a small
bowl. Pat other half flat.

Place filling on half the patty, and cover with the other half of patty. Pinch seams together. Place on a baking tray. Repeat for each ball.

Bake 375 degrees F for 35–40 minutes until sizzling. Serve with plain yogurt on the side.

Lamb Balls—Kafta

Serves 6

- 2 pounds ground lamb or beef
- 1 1/2 cup fresh curly parsley, finely chopped
- 3–4 green onions, finely chopped
- 1 teaspoon salt
- 1/2 teaspoon pepper
- 1/4 teaspoon cumin

In a large bowl, mix all ingredients thoroughly. Form into an oval as pictured. Cook over the barbecue 3 minutes on each side. Serve with salad, vegetables, and plain yogurt on the side.

Turkey and Sausage Meatloaf

Serves 6

- 1 pound ground turkey
- 1/2 pound pork sausage
- 1/2 cup panko or bread crumbs
- 1 large egg
- 1 teaspoon salt
- 1 teaspoon pepper
- 1 teaspoon granulated garlic
- 1 teaspoon granulated onion
- 1 teaspoon cumin

In a large bowl, mix all ingredients. Gently pat into a lightly oiled 8x8-inch baking dish. Prior to baking, cut in traditional diamond cut (refer to pictures at the beginning of chapter). Bake at 350 degrees F for 30–35 minutes until the edges are brown. After baking, place on tray and serve.

This food is economical, which helps fit our retired budget.

Green Beans and Lamb—Loubi bi Lahm

Serves 6

- 2 pounds lamb shanks or chuck roast
- 3 tablespoons olive oil
- 1 large dry yellow onion, diced
- 3 cloves garlic, minced
- 1 teaspoon salt
- 1 teaspoon pepper
- 1 teaspoon dried oregano
- 1 teaspoon dried parsley flakes
- 1 teaspoon dried basil
- 1 pound fresh green beans
- 2 cups water
- 8-ounce can tomato sauce

In a 10-quart pot, brown meat in oil. Add onion, garlic, salt, pepper, oregano, parsley and basil. Sauté until onions are transparent. Add beans, water, and tomato sauce.

Cover, bring to boil, and reduce heat to medium low. Simmer 2 hours until meat is tender. Using two forks, break stewed meat into chunks. Put meat and beans in a serving dish and the extra sauce on the side. Serve with Steamed Rice.

Just imagine there are onions and garlic cloves in this. After I started the meat, I cut my thumb on the lid of an open can, and I couldn't cut the onions and peel the garlic. I substituted 1 tablespoon granulated garlic and 1 tablespoon onion powder. It was still really good. Also, be careful not to burn your wrist from the steam when lifting the lid. This is a basic Lebanese recipe that Mom made a lot. For variety, substitute any vegetable for the green beans. This recipe is healthy and economical.

Chuck's Stuffed Zucchini with Tomato Sauce–Kusa Mihshi Bi Bandoura

Serves 5–6

Traditionally, wider pale green zucchini with tender skin is used for kusa. My mother was always very careful when handling these. Mom used to grow what she called white zucchini. Pictured here is Mexican grey squash. It is very close to Mom's white zucchini. This recipe comes from my brother Chuck, retired teacher who makes great kusa.

For the Meat

- 4 lamb shoulder cuts, riblets, or chops
- 2 tablespoons olive oil
- 3 cloves garlic, minced, divided
- 1/2 cup dry yellow onion, finely chopped

For the Zucchini and Stuffing

- 8–10 zucchini, 6 inches in length
- 1 cup uncooked white rice
- 1 pound medium or coarsely ground lamb or beef
- 15-ounce can diced tomatoes or 4 fresh tomatoes, diced
- 2 tablespoons fresh curly parsley, finely chopped
- 2 teaspoons salt, divided
- 1 teaspoon dried oregano
- 1 teaspoon dried basil
- 1 teaspoon paprika
- 1 teaspoon pepper, divided

For the Cooking Pot Soup

- 15-ounce can tomato sauce
- enough water to cover kusa while cooking
- 1/4 teaspoon allspice
- 1 cup pine nuts, optional

In a 12-quart pot, brown lamb bones with 2 tablespoons olive oil. Add 2 cloves minced garlic and the onion. Reduce heat to low and simmer while preparing zucchini and stuffing.

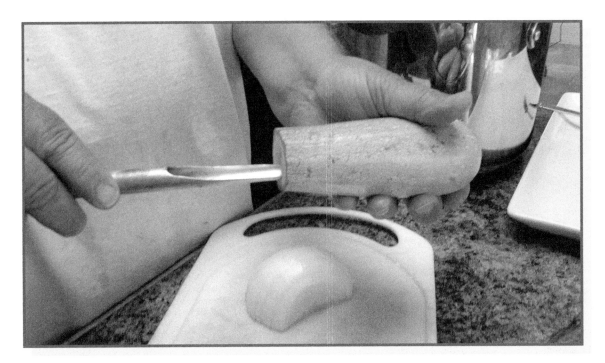

For the Zucchini and Stuffing

Wash and cut stem end off. Core zucchini at room temperature leaving 1/2-inch wall, place in cold water, and drain when ready to use. Into a large bowl, place the rice, lamb or beef, diced tomatoes, parsley, I teaspoon salt, oregano, basil, paprika, and 1/2 teaspoon pepper. If desired, chop some of the hollowed-out zucchini and add to stuffing. Mix well. Stuff the zucchini with the meat mixture. Start by putting a little in and tapping it down. Finish stuffing zucchini. Do not pack tightly as to allow space for the rice to expand. Stuff all zucchini and set aside while preparing the Cooking Pot Soup.

For the Cooking Pot Soup:

Pour tomato sauce in pan with cooked lamb bones. If desired, chop some of the hollowed out zucchini and add to pot. Arrange the stuffed zucchini in pot. Cover zucchini with water. Add 1 teaspoon salt, 1/2 teaspoon pepper, allspice, and remaining garlic clove. If you have leftover stuffing, you can add it to pot. Cook over medium heat 45—50 minutes, just until the zucchini is tender and the rice is cooked.

Remove zucchini from pan with two spoons. Cut zucchini open and pour sauce over.

Larry's Easy Pot of Kusa

All you need to do is slice the zucchini in wheels, put all the ingredients in a pot, bring to boil, reduce heat to low, and let stew 45–50 minutes. Be careful not to put too much rice in, or it will take over. Cut the amount of rice in half.

Sally's Rolled Grape Leaves

Serves 6–8

- 50 grape leaves, fresh or canned
- 2 cups medium or coarse ground or finely diced lamb or beef
- 1 cup uncooked white rice
- 1/2 teaspoon allspice
- salt and pepper to taste
- 1 pound lamb shoulder cuts, riblets, or chops
- water
- 1/4 cup lemon juice

Wash fresh leaves in hot water to wilt or freeze and thaw leaves. If leaves are canned, rinse with cold water to remove salt. In a large bowl, mix ground meat, rice, allspice, salt, and pepper, keeping the mixture loose. Place a tablespoon of mixture along edge of back side of leaf. Roll once, turn sides in, and finish rolling.

The proper way to roll grape leaves.

Place a tablespoon mixture along edge of back side of leaf.

 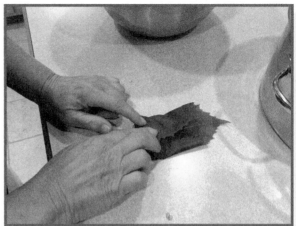

Roll once, and turn the sides in

Finish rolling, and place a few leaves in bottom of a 10-quart pot. Add shoulder cuts, riblets, or chops. Arrange rolled grape leaves tightly in pan side by side to prevent opening.

Place small lid or pottery plates on top of grape leaves to keep them from opening when cooking. Cover completely with water. Cover pan, bring to a boil, reduce heat to low, and cook 15 minutes. Add lemon juice, and cook another 15 minutes. Turn into serving bowl. Serve with plain yogurt.

Meatless Rolled Grape Leaves

Serves 5-6

- 1 1/2 cups uncooked white rice
- 3/4 cup fresh curly parsley, finely chopped
- 6 green onions, finely chopped
- 2 medium tomatoes, seeded and chopped
- 1 teaspoon salt
- 1/2 teaspoon pepper
- About 40 grape leaves

In a medium bowl, mix rice, parsley, onions, tomato, salt, and pepper. Prepare the same as grape leaves with meat, except roll the leaves a little looser to allow the rice to expand.

Mom liked Swiss chard and occasionally used it instead of grape leaves. Wilt the leaves by dipping them in hot water for 30 seconds. Slice each leaf in half at the rib, and remove hard rib. Prepare as you would meatless grape leaves.

Rolled Cabbage Leaves—Mihshi Malfuf

Serves 6-8

- 1 medium head cabbage
- 1 cup uncooked white rice
- 1 pound medium- or coarse-ground lamb or beef
- 2 teaspoons salt, divided
- 1/2 teaspoon pepper
- 1/2 teaspoon allspice
- 1/4 cup lemon juice
- 4–5 lamb riblets, optional
- 1 teaspoon granulated garlic

Wash and core cabbage. In a large pot, bring enough water to boil to completely cover the cabbage. When boiling, carefully lower cabbage into pot using something to support the cabbage. I use a very large spoon. Bring to boil again. Being careful not to tear leaves, use tongs to peel leaves free of head. Keep peeling leaves away as they wilt. It takes about 3 minutes for the leaves to wilt enough to roll. As they wilt, remove from pot and set aside. Continue until all leaves are wilted.

Use the dark green outer leaves to line the bottom of the cooking pot. Slice remaining leaves in half on rib and trim off rib. Leaves from the outside of the cabbage will be larger than the inner leaves. The cabbage rolls will vary slightly in size. When cabbage leaves are ready, mix rice, meat, 1 teaspoon salt, pepper, and allspice in a medium bowl.

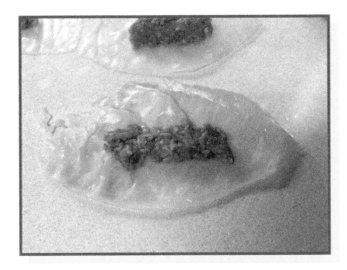 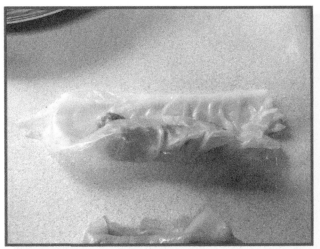

Place tablespoon of mixture on each leaf. Spread lengthwise, and roll. Wrap leaf around meat mixture.

 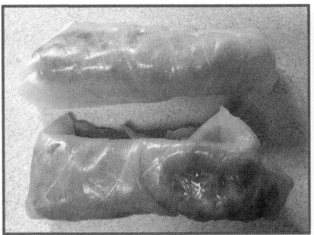

Fold sides of leaf in. Finish rolling. Gently squeeze each roll. Place in 10-quart pot, seam side down. Arrange in compact rows over a layer of lamb riblets if using. I like my cabbage without riblets.

Add 1 teaspoon salt and 1 teaspoon granulated garlic. Cover cabbage rolls with water.

Cover cabbage with cooking lid or pottery plate to keep cabbage together.

Bring to boil, reduce heat to medium low, cover pot, and cook 40 minutes.

Lebanese Baked Chicken with Rice Dressing

Serves 6

We have rice dressing often with chicken.

- *1 whole chicken, 4–5 pounds*
- *2 tablespoons softened butter*
- *1 teaspoon salt*
- *1 teaspoon cumin*
- *1 teaspoon garlic*
- *1/2 teaspoon pepper*
- *1 recipe Rice Dressing*

Wash chicken and pat dry with paper towels. Combine the next five ingredients, and smear spice rub all over chicken and under the skin. I use a toothpick to secure the skin where it was loosened. Place in roasting pan. Bake at 400 degrees F for 55–60 minutes.

Serve chicken in pieces over a platter of Rice Dressing.

Skewered Barbeque Chicken–Shish Tawook

Serves 2

- 2 half boneless chicken breasts,
  each cut into 5 or 6 even pieces
- 3 tablespoons canola oil
- 2 cloves finely minced garlic
- salt and pepper to taste
- 1/2 teaspoon curry powder, optional
- 1/2 sweet white onion,
  cut into chunks
- 1/2 green and red pepper,
  cut into chunks

Cut two boneless chicken breasts into 5 or 6 even pieces. Place chicken in plastic zip-top bag. Add canola oil, garlic, salt and pepper, and curry powder (if using). Marinate in refrigerator at least two hours. Place chicken and vegetables on skewers, and grill 3 or 4 minutes on each side (12–16 minutes total). This is great with salad, hummus, and rice. Leg of lamb or beef sirloin is also great prepared this way.

The closer the meat is to room temperature when cooked, the less moisture is lost in cooking. Take steaks and roasts out of the refrigerator 30 minutes prior to cooking.

Meatless Fried Bean Cakes - Falafel

Makes 10

- 1 cup dried fava beans
- 1 cup dried chickpeas
- 1 medium white or yellow onion, chopped
- 1/2 cup fresh curly parsley, chopped
- 3 cloves garlic, peeled and cut in half
- 3 tablespoons all-purpose flour
- 1 teaspoon baking soda
- 1/2 teaspoon freshly ground pepper
- 1/2 teaspoon ground cumin
- 1/2 teaspoon ground coriander
- 1/2 teaspoon cayenne pepper
- peanut oil for frying

Rinse and soak fava beans in 3 cups of water 48 hours, changing water each day. Rinse and soak chickpeas in 3 cups water for 15 hours. Drain beans. After soaking, remove the skins from the fava beans. Squeeze bean firmly, and it should pop out of its skin. If not, slit skin with knife to remove bean. Sometimes, beans are available already skinned.

Place all ingredients except oil into food processor. Pulse until dough forms. Let stand 1 hour. Take 1/4-cup quantities of dough, and shape into flat patties. Deep fry in 375 degrees F hot peanut oil until brown on both sides. Serve hot with tomato wedges and hummus.

Pocket Bread and Things Made with Pocket Bread

Growing up, we ate mostly pocket bread, also called pita or Middle East bread. It wasn't available in stores in the 1950s and 1960s, so we made it at home. Mom had a special oven just for baking pocket bread. Much like a pizza oven, it could heat to higher temperatures than a conventional oven. Since there were 11 of us, we made a lot of bread. I remember making 70-80 loaves of pocket bread once a week. What a project. I would be up to my elbows kneading dough. Just kneading that much dough was a major effort. It was tough work. Baking bread took all day. Everyone in the neighborhood could smell it. When we baked, our friends would start showing up at the door.

Pocket Bread

Serves 8

- 1 1/4 cups water
- 1 tablespoon yeast
- 1 teaspoon salt
- 1 teaspoon sugar
- 4 cups all-purpose flour

Put a little hot water in a metal or glass bowl, and roll it around to warm up the bowl. Pour water out. Put 1 1/4 cups warm water in bowl and dissolve yeast.

Let stand a few minutes until the yeast becomes active. Add salt and sugar and dissolve. Add flour 1 cup at a time, stir together, and knead dough until sticky. This will take approximately 5 minutes.

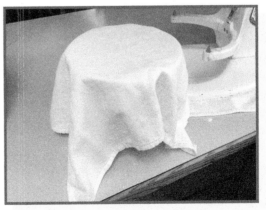

Cover dough with cloth, set in warm place, and let rise 2 hours or until double in size.

Put dough on floured surface, and cut into 8 pieces. Using your floured hands, roll each loaf into a ball, and set on floured waxed paper. Cover with cloth, and let rise 20–30 minutes. When the dough finishes rising the second time, preheat oven to highest baking temperature. Conventional ovens reach 550 degrees F. Convection ovens reach 500 degrees F.

 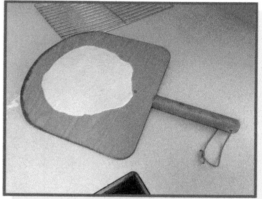

Pat around the edge of the loaf, avoiding the center. Gently roll with a rolling pin. To keep the center of loaf from becoming too thin, always roll from the center out. Place on bread shovel, being careful not to tear or poke a hole in the dough. My brother Larry made each of us one of the bread shovels shown.

Carefully slide onto the middle rack of oven. Close door quickly. Set timer for 2 1/2 minutes. Bread will pop open in a big ball while baking. As soon as you see any browning at all, remove loaf from oven. Be very careful of the steam inside the bread. It will scald you. Place on cooling rack.

Lamb Pies–Fatayer Bi Lahm

Serves 12

- 1 Pocket Bread dough recipe
- 1 pound lean lamb, coarsely ground
- 1/2 cup pine nuts
- 1 medium onion, finely chopped
- 1/4 cup fresh lemon juice
- 1/2 teaspoon salt
- 1/2 teaspoon pepper

Make pocket bread recipe. Prior to the second rise, divide dough into 4 pieces. While bread dough is on the second rise, combine remaining ingredients for the filling. Allow loaves to rise 20 minutes until doubled in size. Pizza dough in the cold case at the grocery store can be substituted for homemade dough.

When dough is ready, preheat oven to 375 degrees F. Roll dough into pie crust thickness. Cut 4-inch rounds. I use the lid from my small saucepan. Pick up leftover dough, and roll into ball for reuse. This is my niece rolling the dough. My great niece also helped to roll dough, cut rounds, and pinch seams, passing this traditional family recipe to another generation.

Place 2 tablespoons filling in the center of each round, and spread not quite to the side. Bring 3 equal points together above center of filling. Tightly pinch three seams together to seal. Place 2 inches apart on greased sheet pan. Bake 20 minutes. Cool on racks.

Spinach Pies—Fatayer Sbanikh

Serves 12

Fatayer Sbanikh, my personal favorite.
These are prepared just like Fatayer with
lamb, just with a different filling. These
are filled with a wonderful spinach salad.

- *1 Pocket Bread dough recipe*
- *2 bunches fresh spinach, washed and cut into 1-inch pieces*
- *6 green onions, finely chopped*
- *1/2 cup vegetable or canola oil*
- *1/2 cup fresh lemon juice*
- *1 bunch fresh curly parsley, finely chopped*
- *salt and pepper to taste*

While bread dough is rising, mix remaining ingredients together. Pizza dough in the cold case at the grocery store can be substituted for homemade dough. Prior to the second rise, divide dough into 4 loaves. Allow loaves to rise 20 minutes until doubled in size. When bread dough is ready, roll dough into pie crust thickness. Cut 4-inch rounds. I use the lid from my small saucepan to cut the dough into rounds. Pick up leftover dough, and roll into ball for reuse. Place 2 tablespoons filling in the center of each round, and spread not quite to the sides. Be careful not to get juice on the sides of the round. Use a little flour on your fingers to help pinch the seams together. Bring 3 equal points together above center of filling. Pinch 3 seams together to seal. Place 2 inches apart on greased sheet pan. Bake at 375 degrees F for 25 minutes. Cool on rack.

Sometimes, I put 1/2 cup crumbled feta cheese in these. It is not traditional, but it is tasty!

Open-Face Meat Pies—Sfiha

- 1 Pocket Bread dough recipe
- 2 tablespoons olive oil
- 1 pound lean lamb or beef, coarsely ground
- 2 white or yellow onions, finely chopped
- 1/2 cup pine nuts
- 3 fresh mint leaves, finely chopped
- 1/2 teaspoon salt
- 1/4 teaspoon allspice
- 1/4 teaspoon black pepper
- 1/4 teaspoon white pepper
- 1 cup plain yogurt

Make Pocket Bread dough. Pizza dough in the cold case at the grocery store can be substituted for homemade dough. While dough is rising, brown lamb, onion, and pine nuts in olive oil. Add seasonings and mint. When meat is cooked, add yogurt. Refrigerate until dough is ready.

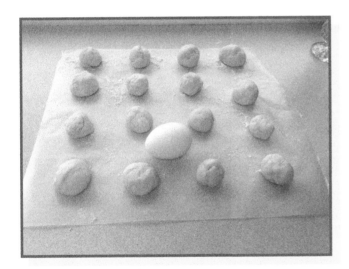

When bread dough is ready, cut into 12 pieces. Form each piece of dough into a ball. Cover with cloth. Let rise on floured surface 20–30 minutes. Roll each ball of dough into a flat round.

Spread 2 tablespoons filling on each round. Wet the edge of the round with finger to help crimping stay together. Pinch them on the edges to give them a crimped edge. Place on a buttered baking sheet or silicone pad. Bake at 375 degrees F for 15–18 minutes.

One more thing made with pocket bread is Zata. You will find the recipe for it in the Appetizers section.

Actually, there is a lot more than just one more thing that you can do with pocket bread. I could probably write an entire book on that. This is a remake of Mom's cookbook of Lebanese and family favorites, so I'm sticking with that for now.

Casseroles, Soups, and Stews

Baked Chicken and Rice Casserole

Serves 6

- 2 cups uncooked white rice
- 8–10 sliced mushrooms or 11-ounce can of sliced mushrooms, drained
- 4 cups chicken broth
- 2 cloves garlic, minced
- 1/2 teaspoon salt
- 1/4 teaspoon cinnamon
- 1/4 teaspoon allspice
- paprika to taste
- pepper to taste
- 1 1/2 whole chicken, cut into pieces
- 2 tablespoons butter

Butter an 11x15-inch baking dish. Spread rice and mushrooms in dish. Mix broth, garlic, salt, cinnamon, and allspice, and pour over rice. Arrange chicken on top, and sprinkle with paprika and pepper. Bake uncovered at 375 degrees F for 1 hour or until chicken is cooked and liquid is absorbed. This is a delicious and easy meal.

Supreme Chicken Casserole

Serves 8

- 2 boneless whole chicken breasts
- 1 teaspoon seasoning salt
- 2 cups uncooked elbow macaroni
- 1 1/2 cups cheddar cheese cubes
- 6 ounces smoked Gouda cheese, cut into small cubes
- 8-ounce can sliced mushrooms, drained
- 1/2 small dry yellow onion, finely diced
- 1 cup milk
- 4 cups chicken broth
- 10.5-ounce can cream of mushroom soup
- 2 cups bread crumbs, cornflake crumbs, or panko
- 2 tablespoons melted butter

Place chicken in a 2-quart saucepan, add seasoning salt, and barely cover chicken with water. Bring to boil, cover, reduce heat to low, and simmer 20 minutes.

Strain chicken, saving broth to use in casserole. Cool and dice chicken.

Place macaroni, cheeses, mushrooms, and onion in a 9x13-inch buttered baking dish. In an 8-cup mixing bowl, whisk together milk, broth, and soup. Pour into baking dish. Cover and let stand in refrigerator at least 6 hours. It can be left overnight. Remove casserole from refrigerator an hour before baking. Bake uncovered 350 degrees F for 50 minutes until hot and bubbly.

Remove from oven. Mix butter with crumbs or panko and sprinkle over top. Return to oven, and bake 15 minutes longer. This is such a great fall dinner, tasty even without chicken.

Wild Rice Casserole

This is so creamy and good.

- 2 cups water or chicken broth
- 1 tablespoon butter
- 1/2 cup uncooked wild rice
- 1/2 cup uncooked white rice
- 1/2 cup celery, finely diced
- 1/2 cup carrots, finely diced
- 2 green onions, diced
- 2 cups cooked chicken, diced
- 1 cup asiago cheese, diced
- 1 cup medium cheddar cheese, diced
- 4 pieces crispy bacon, chopped, or 1 cup diced ham
- 8-ounce can sliced water chestnuts, drained
- 1 cup cooked small shrimp
- 10.5-ounce can cream of mushroom soup
- 10.5-ounce can cream of celery soup
- 2 1/2 cups milk
- 1/4 teaspoon curry powder

Put water or broth and butter in a 4-quart saucepan. Bring to boil. Add rice, celery, carrots, and green onions. Reduce heat to low, cover, and simmer 20 minutes. While rice is cooking, cut chicken, cheese, and bacon. Set aside. When rice is cooked, place in a 9x13-inch buttered baking dish. Layer chicken, cheese, bacon, water chestnuts, and shrimp over rice. In a large bowl, mix soups, milk, and curry powder. Pour mixture over rice. Bake uncovered at 375 degrees F 35–40 minutes until heated through and brown on top.

Lime Jell-O with Mint Pears makes a nice complement to this casserole.

Chicken and Crab Delight

Serves 4

- 4 boneless half chicken breasts
- 4 tablespoons butter, divided
- 1/4 cup all-purpose flour
- 2 cups milk
- 1/4 teaspoon tarragon
- 1 pound fresh crab

Preheat oven to 350 degrees F.

Cut chicken breasts into three pieces as shown below.

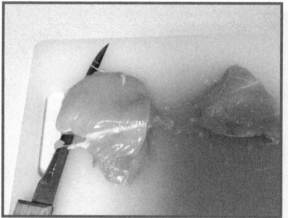

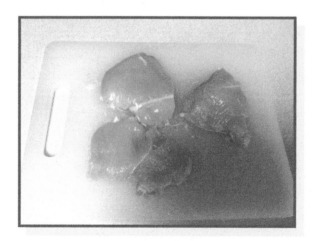

Place chicken in a 9x13-inch buttered baking dish. On medium heat, melt 3 tablespoons butter in saucepan. Stir flour into butter. Cook three minutes. Slowly add milk and tarragon, stirring constantly. Remove from heat, transfer to a bowl and rinse pan. In the same saucepan, cook crab in remaining butter and add cream sauce. Pour crab mixture over chicken. Bake 20 minutes.

Mashed Potato Casserole and Stuffed Potatoes

Ever want something easy for leftover mashed or baked potatoes? Here are two recipes that use the same meat mixture.

Meat Mixture

- 1/4 cup pine nuts
- 1 tablespoon butter
- 1 pound ground lamb or beef
- 1/2 teaspoon salt
- 1/4 teaspoon pepper
- 1/4 teaspoon allspice
- 10.5-ounce can cream of mushroom soup
- 1 cup water
- 3 green onions, chopped

In a 10-inch skillet over medium-high heat, sauté pine nuts in butter until brown. Watch them closely, so they don't burn. Remove and set aside. In the same skillet, add meat, salt, pepper and allspice. Cook until meat is brown. Drain fat Add soup, water, onions, and pine nuts. Stir until warm.

Mashed Potato Casserole

Serves 6

Spread 2 cups mashed potatoes in 8x8-inch buttered baking dish. Spread meat mixture on top. Add 2 more cups mashed potato on top. Bake covered at 375 degrees F for 25 minutes.

Stuffed Potatoes

Serves 2

- 2 potatoes
- 1/2 cup shredded Colby jack cheese
- 2 tomatoes, diced

Wash and pierce potatoes. Wrap in foil. Bake potatoes at 400 degrees F for 50–60 minutes until tender. Allow to cool at least 1 hour. Cut potatoes in half lengthwise and hollow the center. Stuff potatoes with meat mixture. Sprinkle with cheese and tomatoes.

Place potatoes in a 9x13-inch buttered baking dish. Bake at 375 degrees F for 35–40 minutes. Try adding 1/2 cup peas; finely diced carrots; or red, yellow, or green pepper.

Hamburger Noodle Casserole

Serves 8

Pictured with Parmesan chips

- 1 1/2 pounds ground beef
- 1 sweet white onion, diced
- 10.5-ounce can cream of mushroom soup
- 10.5-ounce can cream of celery soup
- 8-ounce can tomato sauce
- 2 cups milk
- 15.5-ounce can sliced mushrooms, drained
- 1 teaspoon granulated garlic
- 1 teaspoon salt
- 1/2 teaspoon white pepper
- 12 ounces egg noodles
- 1/2 cup grated Parmesan cheese

In a 10-inch skillet over medium-high heat, sauté beef and onion. Add soup, tomato sauce, mushrooms, garlic, salt, white pepper, and milk. Set aside. Cook noodles according to package directions. In a 9x13-inch buttered baking dish, layer half the noodles, half the meat mixture, the remaining noodles, and the remaining meat mixture. Sprinkle cheese over casserole. Bake covered at 350 degrees F for 40 minutes. Uncover and bake for 10 more minutes. This can be made the day ahead and baked when ready. Remove from refrigerator 30 minutes before baking.

Simple Casserole for Two

Serves 2

I try to reinvent leftovers, so my husband will eat them.

- 4 ounces egg noodles
- 8-ounce can tomato sauce
- 1/2 cup ranch dressing
- 1/2 pound or so leftover meatloaf or cooked ground meat
- 2 tablespoons grated Parmesan cheese

Cook noodles according to package directions. In a small bowl, mix tomato sauce and ranch dressing. Layer half the noodles in a 7x 5-inch buttered baking dish. Sprinkle half the meat over the noodles and then half the sauce mixture. Repeat and top with Parmesan cheese. Bake covered 375 degrees F for 25 minutes. Uncover, and bake 10 more minutes until hot and bubbly.

Layered Eggplant and Lamb–A Royal Dish

Serves 6

- 1 pound leg of lamb or beef sirloin steak, finely diced or coarsely ground
- 1 dry yellow onion, chopped
- 1/4 cup pine nuts
- 1 teaspoon salt
- 1/2 teaspoon pepper
- 1/2 teaspoon allspice
- 2 tablespoon butter, divided
- 1 eggplant, peeled and sliced into 1/2-inch pieces
- 15.5-ounce can tomato sauce or diced tomatoes
- In a 10-inch skillet, sauté first six ingredients in 1 tablespoon butter until lightly brown. Set aside.

Fry eggplant lightly in 1 tablespoon butter (or grill). Arrange half the eggplant in 8x8-inch buttered baking dish. Layer meat mixture, and add remaining eggplant. Pour tomato sauce over casserole and enough water to barely cover the top. If desired, sprinkle on a little more salt and pepper. Bake uncovered at 375 degrees F for 40 minutes until bubbly. Serve with Steamed Rice.

Stuffed Eggplant–Sheikh Al Mihshi

Serves 6

- 2 eggplant
- 1 pound leg of lamb or beef sirloin steak, finely diced or coarsely ground
- 1/2 cup pine nuts
- 2 tablespoons fresh curly parsley, finely chopped
- 1 teaspoon salt
- 1/2 teaspoon pepper
- 28-ounce can tomato sauce or 6 diced tomatoes, divided
- 3 cups water
- 1 teaspoon salt
- 1/2 teaspoon pepper
- 1/2 teaspoon allspice
- 1 clove garlic, minced

Cut eggplant in half lengthwise, and use a spoon to hollow the center, leaving a 1/2-inch wall. In a mixing bowl, combine meat, pine nuts, parsley, salt, pepper, and half the tomatoes. Mix well. Stuff the eggplant with the meat mixture. Place in 11x15-inch buttered baking dish. Pour remaining tomatoes and water in pan. Add salt, pepper, allspice, and garlic. Bake uncovered at 375 degrees for 45 minutes. Carefully remove eggplant from pan with two spoons, and pour sauce over eggplant.

Chicken and Couscous Soup–Moughrabieh

Makes 10 cups soup and 2 cups couscous

This is my dad's favorite comfort food. I like it too. Traditionally, this also has lamb, but we prefer just the chicken in this soup.

For the Soup
- 2 boneless half chicken breasts
- 8 cups chicken broth
- 1 sweet white onion, cut into large chunks
- 4 cloves garlic, smashed with flat side of knife
- 1 teaspoon salt
- 1 teaspoon white pepper
- 15.5-ounce can garbanzo beans, drained
- 1/2 teaspoon cinnamon

For the Couscous
- 1 cup couscous
- 2 tablespoons butter
- 1 1/4 cups hot water

For the Soup
In a 4-quart saucepan, place chicken, broth, onion, garlic, salt, and pepper. Cover pot, and bring to a boil over high heat. Reduce heat to low, and simmer 20 minutes. Strain broth. Discard onion and garlic. Using two forks, shred chicken into spoon-sized pieces. Return broth and chicken to pot. Add garbanzo beans and cinnamon. Return to heat and simmer while preparing couscous.

For the Couscous

In a 2-quart saucepan, brown couscous in butter stirring constantly until golden brown.

When golden, add 1 1/4 cups hot water. Be careful. It will steam. Cook 10–12 minutes, stirring occasionally. When cooked, place 1/4 cup couscous in the bottom of a soup bowl. Pour the soup over the couscous.

Meatless Lentil and Rice Soup

Makes 4 quarts

- 1 1/2 cups dried lentils, uncooked
- 2 medium dry white onions
- 2 tablespoons canola oil
- 3 tablespoons butter
- 7 cups water
- 1 teaspoon salt
- 1/2 cup uncooked white rice

Rinse and sort lentils. Peel and thinly slice onions in into half-moons. In a 5-quart pot, sauté onion in oil and butter until transparent. Add lentils, water and salt. Bring to boil. Reduce heat to low and stir in rice. Cover and simmer 20 minutes. This can be made without the rice. Serve with a dollop of plain yogurt. This soup freezes beautifully.

Lamb, Rice, and Yogurt Soup—Lubin Imu

Serves 6

- 2 quarts water
- 2 teaspoons salt
- 4 lamb shanks
- 1 large bay leaf
- 1 teaspoons granulated garlic
- 1 teaspoons granulated onion
- 2 cups plain yogurt
- 1 cup uncooked white rice

Boil 2 quarts salted water in a 10-quart pot. Add lamb shanks, bay leaf, granulated garlic, and granulated onion, and return to a boil. Reduce heat to low, and simmer two hours or until meat falls off the bone. Discard bones, and break meat into small pieces. Skim fat from broth, and discard bay leaf. Add meat, rice, and yogurt to broth. Bring to gentle boil, and reduce heat. Simmer on medium-low heat, stirring occasionally, until rice is cooked (approximately 15 minutes). Serve with salad and a soft roll.

Lamb Shank and Kidney Bean Soup

Makes 3 quarts

So good on a cold, rainy day.

- *2 lamb shanks*
- *1 dry yellow onion, cut into large chunks*
- *2 cloves garlic, smashed with flat side of knife*
- *1 teaspoon salt*
- *1/2 teaspoon pepper*
- *15.5-ounce can kidney beans, rinsed well*
- *15.5-ounce can tomato sauce*
- *2 tablespoons dried parsley*
- *1 tablespoons dried oregano*
- *1 tablespoons dried basil*

In a 4-quart saucepan, place lamb shanks and cover with water. Add onion, garlic, salt, and pepper. Bring to boil, reduce heat to low, cover, and simmer two hours until lamb is tender enough to remove from the bone. Strain liquid, and skim fat. Discard onion and garlic. Break lamb into spoon-sized pieces, and discard bones. Return lamb and stock to pot with remaining ingredients. Simmer 30 minutes. Serve over rice or as a soup. Leftovers freeze well.

Easy Stove-Top Steamed Rice and Lamb

Serves 6

- *4 tablespoons butter*
- *1 pound leg of lamb or beef sirloin steak, finely diced or coarsely ground*
- *1/2 cup dry yellow onion, chopped*
- *1/2 cup celery, chopped*
- *2 cups uncooked white rice*
- *1/2 cup slivered almonds*
- *1 3/4 cups hot beef broth*

In a 4-quart saucepan, melt butter and sauté meat on medium-high heat in butter until brown. Add onion and celery. Cook until onion is translucent. Add remaining ingredients. Bring to a boil, reduce heat to low, cover, and cook 20 minutes.

Lamb and Summer Vegetable Stew

Makes 4 quarts

- 2 tablespoons olive oil
- 4 lamb shoulder cuts or blade steaks
- 2 quarts water
- 1/2 teaspoon salt
- 1/4 teaspoon pepper
- 1/4 teaspoon allspice
- 1 dry yellow onion, diced
- 2 cloves garlic, minced fine
- 1 eggplant, peeled and cut into
  2-inch cubes
- 2 medium zucchini, thickly sliced
- 15-ounce can diced tomatoes

In a 10-quart pot, heat oil over medium-high heat, and brown lamb on both sides. Add water, salt, pepper and allspice. Bring to boil, cover, and reduce heat to low. Simmer 90 minutes until meat falls off bones. Remove lamb from broth. Separate bones and meat. Discard bones. Using two forks, break meat into small pieces. Skim fat from broth. Return meat to broth. Add remaining ingredients, and bring to gentle boil. Reduce heat to low, cover, and simmer 30 minutes. Excellent over Steamed Rice with Vermicelli or with a hard roll.

Lamb and Barley Stew—Harisseh

Makes 6 quarts

My sister Sally made this wonderful
stew.

- 4 lamb shanks or shoulder cuts
- 3 tablespoons olive oil
- 2 dry yellow onions, chopped
- 1 tablespoon cumin
- 1 teaspoon salt
- 1/2 teaspoon pepper
- 1/2 teaspoon cinnamon
- 11 cups water, divided
- 1 1/2 cups whole-grain barley

In a 10-quart pot, brown lamb in oil. Add onion, cumin, salt, pepper, cinnamon, and 8 cups water. Bring to boil. Reduce heat to low, cover, and simmer about 2 hours or until meat is tender. In a separate bowl, cover barley with 3 cups water.

When lamb is tender, remove to a large plate, and separate lamb from the bones. Return lamb to pot, and discard bones. Drain barley and add to pot. Bring to slow boil, and cook 1 hour or until barley is tender. If it becomes too dry while cooking, just add a little water.

This is a great stew. It is delicious and hearty.

Desserts

Hints for good baked goods: Measurements are important. Always use liquid measuring cups for wet ingredients and dry measuring cups for dry ingredients. Use a flat surface such as the back of a knife to level the measurements. Do not scoop flour with measuring cup. You can pack the flour and get too much. Fluff flour with a fork before putting it in a measuring cup. For best results, ingredients should be between 68 and 70 degrees unless otherwise stated!

Best-Ever Carrot Cake

For Cake

- 2 cups all-purpose flour, sifted
- 2 teaspoons baking soda
- 1 teaspoons cinnamon
- 1 teaspoon allspice
- 1/2 teaspoon salt
- 1/4 teaspoon nutmeg
- 1/4 teaspoon ground cloves
- 20-ounce can crushed pineapple, drained, juice reserved and save juice
- 4 eggs
- 2 cups sugar
- 1 1/2 cups canola oil
- 3 cups grated carrots
- 1 cup chopped slivered almonds
- 3/4 cup white raisins

For Coconut and Pineapple Frosting

- 1 cup shredded coconut
- 1/2 cup milk
- 1/3 cup all-purpose flour
- 1/2 cup reserved pineapple juice
- 1 cup butter, room temperature
- 1 cup sugar
- 1 tsp. vanilla extract

For the Cake

Preheat oven to 350 degrees F. Sift flour, baking soda, salt, and spices in mixing bowl. Set aside. Drain pineapple and save juice. Beat eggs and sugar on medium-high speed until light yellow. Add oil. Mix in dry ingredients on medium-low speed until just combined. Add carrots, almonds, pineapple and raisins. Fold together, and pour into 9x13-inch greased baking dish. Bake 50 minutes or until toothpick comes out clean. When cake is cool, make the frosting.

For the Coconut and Pineapple Frosting

Toast coconut on baking sheet at 350 degrees F for 10–15 minutes, stirring once, until golden brown. This can be done when baking cake. In a 2-quart saucepan, whisk milk and flour until smooth. Whisk in pineapple juice, and cook over medium-high heat until thick and bubbly. Remove from heat, and transfer to a bowl. Cover with plastic wrap to prevent a skin from forming on top. Let stand until room temperature. When cake is completely cool, whip butter and sugar until fluffy. Add vanilla. Add cooked flour mixture, 1 tablespoon at a time, and whip well between each addition. Do not add it too quickly. You will have a light and fluffy icing that isn't too sweet. Spread icing on cake and sprinkle toasted coconut on top. This cake is absolutely irresistible.

My Special Mocha Frosting

Makes enough for an 8x8-inch baking dish

This frosting is light and not too sweet. It is great on cakes and brownies. Pictured are brownies.

- *2 1/2 tablespoon all-purpose flour*
- *1/2 cup milk*
- *1/2 cup butter, room temperature*
- *1/2 cup sugar*
- *1 tablespoon cocoa powder*
- *1 teaspoon instant espresso powder*
- *1/2 teaspoon vanilla extract*

In a small saucepan, whisk flour and milk until smooth. Cook on medium-high heat until thick and beginning to bubble. Stir constantly to avoid scorching. Remove from heat. Put into small bowl and cover with plastic wrap to avoid forming a tough skin. Allow to cool to room temperature. When ready to ice your baked good, cream butter, sugar, cocoa, espresso, and vanilla until completely incorporated. Add milk mixture, 1 tablespoon at a time, and whip on high speed between each addition. Do not add milk mixture too quickly.

When I was in high school, I took a cooking class that focused on budget and time-management. One of the things we did was to compare package mixes with making things from scratch. My group had brownies. The brownie mix was moister, tastier, quicker, and more economical than the one we made from scratch. I found a brownie mix that my husband likes, and I always buy that brand.

That was such a fun class. My mom used to give Lebanese cooking demonstrations at my school every year. She also gave cooking lessons at a place in town called Yankee Kitchen. She was a fantastic cook and an amazing woman.

Snowball Cookies

Makes 2 dozen

My grandmother made these family-favorite cookies for holidays.

- 1 cup butter, room temperature
- 1/2 cup sugar
- 1 egg
- 1 teaspoon vanilla
- 1/2 teaspoon salt
- 3 cups all-purpose flour, sifted
- 3/4 cup finely chopped nuts

Preheat oven to 375 degrees F. In a medium bowl, cream butter and sugar. Add egg, vanilla, and salt. Blend, and add flour, a little at a time. Add nuts. Roll dough into 1 1/2-inch balls, and place on an ungreased cookie sheet. Bake 17–20 minutes until lightly brown on the bottom. Cool, and sprinkle powdered sugar over the top to serve. These are buttery good.

Date or Walnut Crescents

Makes 30 cookies

Traditionally, this is called Ma Mul. It is a date- or walnut-filled cookie made in a special mold. Mom had a Lebanese wooden mold with a design in it. I wish I had it today. Since I don't, I make crescent shaped cookies out of the same dough and filling. It is an easy dough to work and very tasty.

For the Dough
- 3/4 teaspoon yeast
- 1/4 cup lukewarm water
- 1 cup unsalted butter
- 1/3 cup sugar
- 3 cups all-purpose flour
- 1/2 teaspoon salt
- 1/4 cup lukewarm milk

For the Date Filling
- 1 1/2 cups chopped dates
- 1 tablespoon butter, melted

For the Walnut Filling
- 1 1/2 cups walnuts, finely chopped
- 1 cup sugar

For the Dough
Dissolve yeast in water. In a large mixing bowl, cream butter and sugar while allowing the yeast to become active. Add yeast, flour, salt, and milk to creamed mixture. Mix well, kneading into a soft dough. Place in warm spot, cover, and let rise 1 hour.

For the Filling
Choose your filling. Either mix dates with melted butter and microwave 15 seconds or mix walnuts with sugar. Either filling is very good. Mix well and set aside. When dough has set for an hour, preheat oven to 350 degrees F.

On a lightly floured surface, roll dough to 1/4-inch thickness. Cut 2-inch rounds. Gather scrap dough into a ball, and roll to 1/4-inch thickness until all dough is used. Place 1 tablespoon of filling on each round.

Fold top half over the filling, and pinch edges together well. Use a fork or just your fingers, but be sure it is sealed well. Prick the tops. Place on ungreased baking pan. Bake 20 minutes.

My Own Christmas Fudge

Makes 3 pounds

I always think of my brother Larry when
I make this. He loves it.

- 2 (12-ounce) packages semisweet
  chocolate chips
- 8 ounces unsweetened chocolate,
  broken into small pieces
- 1 cup chopped nuts
- 4 cups sugar
- 12-ounce can evaporated milk
- 4 tablespoons butter
- 7-ounce jar marshmallow cream
- 2 ounces mini marshmallows

Grease 9x13-inch pan. Line with waxed paper. In a large bowl, add all chocolate and nuts. Set aside. In a
2-quart saucepan, add sugar, milk, and butter. Bring to a boil over medium heat. Add marshmallow cream
and marshmallows and bring to boil again. Remove from heat, pour over chocolate, and stir until melted. Pour
into prepared pan. Refrigerate until firm.

Rice Pudding

Serves 4

When a new baby is born, it's a Lebanese custom that this pudding is served to guests who come to celebrate with the family.

- 3 cups water
- 1 cup uncooked jasmine rice
- 2 cups milk
- 1 cup sugar
- 1 teaspoon rosewater
- 1 teaspoon cinnamon
- 3/4 cup golden raisins

In a 4-quart saucepan, boil water and add rice. Reduce heat to low, cover, and simmer 15 minutes. Next add milk, sugar, rosewater, and cinnamon. Increase heat to medium. Gently stir until mixture comes to slow boil. Boil until liquid is absorbed. Remove from heat. Add raisins, and pour into serving bowls. This thickens well as it cools.

Other spices may be used: allspice, caraway seed, anise seed, ginger, or nutmeg. Nuts could also be added as well: walnuts, pine nuts, almonds, pecans, or pistachios.

Coconut Cream Pie

All I can say is that this is irresistible. Wow!

For the Filling

- 2 cups shredded coconut
- 5 egg yolks
- 3 cups whole milk
- 1 1/2 cups sugar
- 1/3 cup all-purpose flour
- 1/2 teaspoon salt
- 1/2 cup butter
- 2 teaspoon vanilla extract
- 1 (10-inch) baked pie shell

For the Whipped Topping

- 1 1/2 cups heavy cream
- 1/4 cup powdered sugar
- 1 teaspoon vanilla extract

For the Filling

Toast coconut on baking sheet at 350 degrees F for 10 minutes, stirring once, until lightly brown. Allow to cool while preparing the filling. In a 2 cup bowl, whisk egg yolks until smooth and set aside. In a 6-quart saucepan, whisk the next four ingredients until smooth. Cook on medium-high heat until thick and bubbly, about 3 minutes. Reduce heat to low, and cook 2 minutes, gently stirring constantly. Remove from heat while tempering the egg yolk. To temper the egg yolk, slowly drizzle 1 cup hot mixture into egg yolks, stirring constantly until combined. Slowly pour back into hot mixture, stirring constantly. Return to heat, and bring to gentle boil, stirring constantly. Remove from heat. Stir in butter and vanilla. Save 1/4 cup coconut for the top, and mix the rest into hot mixture. Pour into a 10-inch baked pie shell. Cover with plastic wrap to prevent a tough skin from forming. Be careful not to cover the crust, or it will get soft.

Cool 1 hour at room temperature. Refrigerate until completely chilled, at least 5 hours.

For the Whipped Topping

In a small cold glass bowl, whip cream, powdered sugar, and vanilla on high speed until stiff peaks form. Top pie with whipped topping and remaining coconut. Chill 1 hour.

Chocolate Pudding or Pie Filling

For Pudding or Pie Filling
- 5 egg yolks
- 3 cups whole milk
- 1 1/2 cups sugar
- 1/3 cup all-purpose flour
- 4 tablespoons cocoa powder
- 1/2 teaspoon salt
- 1/2 cup butter
- 2 teaspoon vanilla extract

For the Whipped Topping
- 1 1/2 cups heavy cream
- 1/4 cup powdered sugar
- 1 tsp. vanilla extract

For Pudding or Pie Filling

In a 2-cup bowl, whisk egg yolks until smooth and set aside. In a 6-quart saucepan, whisk next five ingredients until smooth. Cook on medium-high heat until thick and bubbly, about 3 minutes. Reduce heat to low, and cook 2 minutes, gently stirring constantly. Remove from heat while tempering the egg yolk. To temper the egg yolk, slowly drizzle 1 cup hot mixture into egg yolks, stirring constantly until combined. Slowly pour back into hot mixture, stirring constantly. Return to heat, and bring to gentle boil, stirring constantly. Remove from heat. Stir in butter and vanilla. Pour into serving bowl. Cover with plastic wrap to prevent a skin from forming.

Serve warm or chilled with whipped topping on the side.

For Pie

Pour into a 10-inch baked pie shell. Cover with plastic wrap to prevent a tough skin from forming. Be careful not to cover the crust, or it will get soft. Cool 1 hour at room temperature. Refrigerate until completely chilled, at least 5 hours.

For the Whipped Topping

In a small cold glass bowl, whip cream, powdered sugar, and vanilla on high speed until stiff peaks form. Top pie with whipped topping. Chill 1 hour.

Banana Cream with Vanilla Cookies

Leave the bananas out, and you have Vanilla Cream Pudding or Pie Filling.

For the Cream

- 5 egg yolks
- 3 cups whole milk, cold
- 1 1/2 cups sugar
- 1/3 cup all-purpose flour
- 1/2 teaspoon salt
- 1/2 cup butter
- 2 teaspoon vanilla extract
- 2 cups small vanilla cookies
- 2 large bananas

For the Whipped Topping

- 1 1/2 cups heavy cream
- 1/4 cup powdered sugar
- 1 tsp. vanilla extract

In a 2-cup bowl, whisk egg yolks until smooth and set aside. In a 6-quart saucepan, whisk next four ingredients until smooth. Cook on medium-high heat until thick and bubbly, about 3 minutes. Reduce heat to low, and cook 2 minutes gently, stirring constantly. Remove from heat while tempering the egg yolks. To temper the egg yolks, slowly drizzle 1 cup hot mixture into egg yolks, stirring constantly, until combined. Slowly pour back into hot mixture, stirring constantly. Return to heat, and bring to a gentle boil, stirring constantly. Remove from heat. Stir in butter and vanilla. Line bottom and sides of a glass serving bowl or dish with cookies. Slice bananas over cookies. Pour hot mixture over bananas. Cover with plastic wrap to prevent a skin from forming. Cool 1 hour at room temperature and then refrigerate. Can be served warm or cold with whipped topping on the side.

For Pie

Slice bananas into a 10-inch baked pie shell. Pour hot mixture over top. Cover with plastic wrap to prevent a skin from forming. Be careful not to cover the crust, or it will get soft. Cool 1 hour at room temperature, and refrigerate until completely chilled (at least 5 hours).

For the Whipped Topping

In a small cold glass bowl, whip cream, powdered sugar, and vanilla on high speed until stiff peaks form. Top pie with whipped topping. Chill 1 hour.

Pie Crust

Makes 2 single crusts

This pie crust is flaky every time. I have used this recipe for years.

- 3 cups all-purpose flour
- 1 teaspoon salt
- 1 1/4 cups shortening
- 1 large egg
- 1/3 cup cold water
- 1 tablespoon white vinegar

Preheat the oven to 400 degrees F.

In a large bowl, mix flour and salt. Cut shortening into flour, half at a time, until there are pea-sized crumbs. When the shortening melts, this creates a flaky crust.

In a small bowl, mix egg, water, and vinegar. Using a fork, slowly mix liquid mixture into flour mixture until incorporated and the dough forms a ball.

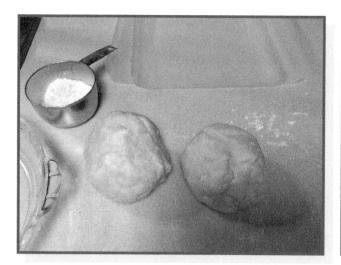 

Divide dough in two, roll into balls, and allow to rest five minutes. Roll balls into 12-inch circles. I roll my dough between 2 sheets of heavily floured waxed paper. It makes it easier to transfer to the pie dish. Place in 10-inch pie dishes. Prick with fork several times, and crimp edges. Bake 12–15 minutes until just golden.

Linda's No-Bake Blueberry Cream Cheese Pie

Serves 12

Another wonderful delight from my sister-in-law Linda.

For the Crust
- 2 cups crushed graham crackers
- 1 1/3 cup powdered sugar, divided
- 1/2 cup melted butter
- 2 (8-ounce) packages cream cheese, softened
- 3 cups blueberries
- 3/4 cup sugar
- 1/4 cup water
- 2 tablespoons cornstarch

For the Whipped Topping
- 1 1/2 cups heavy cream
- 1/4 cup powdered sugar
- 1 tsp. vanilla extract

For the Crust
Combine graham cracker crumbs, 1/3 cup powdered sugar, and melted butter. Press into a 9x13-inch glass dish, and chill while making filling.

For the Filling
Mix cream cheese and remaining powdered sugar until well blended. Using the back of a spoon, spread over chilled crust. Running the spoon under hot water beforehand helps when spreading the cream cheese mixture.

In a 2-quart saucepan, combine berries, sugar, water, and cornstarch. Cook over medium heat until mixture thickens. Cool completely, and pour over cream cheese mixture. This blueberry topping is great on ice cream, shortcake, and in pies.

For the Whipped Topping
In a small cold glass bowl, whip cream, powdered sugar, and vanilla on high speed until stiff peaks form.

Frost with whipped topping, chill, and serve. This recipe freezes well.

Linda's Oatmeal Date Bars

Makes 15

These are my favorite fruit bars.

- 1 1/2 cups all-purpose flour
- 1 1/2 cups oats
- 1 cup brown sugar, packed
- 1/2 teaspoon baking soda
- 3/4 cup butter, room temperature
- 1 pound pitted dates
- 1 cup sugar
- 1 cup water

Preheat oven to 375 degrees F. In large mixing bowl, stir together flour, oats, brown sugar, and baking soda. Using a fork or pastry knife, cut butter into mixture until crumbly.

Pat two-thirds of crumbs into the bottom of ungreased 9x13-inch pan. Reserve the remaining third. In a 2-quart saucepan, cook pitted dates, sugar, and water over medium heat until consistency of jam

Spread mixture over crumbs, top with the remaining crumbs, and bake 25–30 minutes.

Applets

My family grew up in Washington State, the apple capital. We had an abundance of apples from Grandpa's orchard. We climbed trees to pick apples. Then we cooked!

- *1 cup raw apple pulp*
- *2 cups sugar*
- *1 ounce Knox gelatin*
- *5 tablespoons hot water*
- *3/4 cup pecan pieces*
- *2 tablespoons orange juice*
- *1/4 teaspoon lemon zest*

In a 2-quart saucepan, boil apple pulp and sugar until clear. Dissolve gelatin in water. Blend into apple mixture, and add remaining ingredients. Blend together and pour into an ungreased 8x8-inch glass baking dish. Let set up at room temperature. Cut into 2-inch squares, and coat all sides with powdered sugar. Allow to sit uncovered until ready to serve. Coat with sugar again, and place on a dish.

Cake Mix Lemon Bars

Makes 20

- 16.5-ounce box lemon cake mix
- 1/2 cup butter, room temperature
- 4 eggs
- 2 cups sugar
- 6 tablespoons lemon juice
- 4 tablespoons all-purpose flour
- 1 teaspoon baking powder

Preheat oven to 350 degrees F. Lightly grease 9x13-inch baking dish. Mix cake mix and butter until crumbly. Lightly pat into baking dish. Bake 20 minutes. In a small bowl, mix eggs, sugar, lemon juice, flour, and baking powder. Pour over warm crust, and bake another 20 minutes. Cool. Cut into 20 bars, and sprinkle with powdered sugar.

Filo Pastry with Walnuts—Baklawa

My sister Jamilie and her husband, Karl, made this recipe.

- *4 cups walnuts, finely chopped*
- *1 cup sugar*
- *1 pound frozen filo dough*
- *1/2 pound unsalted butter, melted*
- *Basic syrup (see below)*

For the Pastry

Preheat oven to 325 degrees F. Mix walnuts and sugar. Butter a 10x14-inch pan. Unroll filo dough flat, and let relax two minutes. Work quickly so filo does not dry out. Place 3 sheets of filo on bottom of pan, and brush lightly with melted butter. Repeat with 2 sheets of filo and melted butter. Next, layer the nut and sugar mixture. Complete by alternating 2 layers of filo and melted butter until filo is all used. Do not butter the top layer. Cut into traditional diamond cut. Drizzle remaining butter on top. Bake 30 minutes on the middle rack. Increase oven to 425 degrees F and for 5 additional minutes for filo to brown. While in oven, prepare basic syrup. Remove baklawa from oven when golden brown and immediately spoon basic syrup evenly on top. The wet syrup makes the pastry drippier. Most prefer dry syrup. No refrigeration required, store in cool dry place.

Dry Basic Syrup

- *1 cup sugar*
- *1/4 cup water*
- *2 tablespoons lemon juice*

Combine in saucepan to dissolve sugar using low or no heat.

Wet Basic Syrup

- *1 cup water*
- *1 cup sugar*
- *2 tablespoons lemon juice*

Heat in saucepan until all sugar is dissolved. Remove from heat, and let cool.

Variation

- *Ricotta Filling*
- *4 cups ricotta cheese*
- *1 cup sugar*
- *1 egg, beaten*

Combine all ingredients and use for filling in baklawa.

Beirut Lebanon Dessert

Serves 4-6

This is best served hot.

For the Syrup
- 1 cup sugar
- 3/4 cup water
- Zest of 1 lemon

For the Cakes
- 1 1/2 teaspoon yeast
- 1/2 cup warm water
- 1 cup all-purpose flour
- 1/4 cup cornstarch
- 1 tablespoon sugar
- Pinch of salt
- 2 cups vegetable oil

For the Syrup
Combine syrup ingredients in a 2-quart saucepan. Bring to boil over high heat. Boil 15 seconds, and remove from heat. Set aside.

For the Cakes
Dissolve yeast in water. Let sit until bubbly, about 2 minutes. Add remaining ingredients except the oil, and mix thoroughly with a spoon. Cover with clean cloth, and let rise 1 hour.

Pour batter into piping bag with a medium-sized tip. Pour oil into a large skillet, and heat over medium-high heat until oil is moving but not smoking. If the oil isn't hot, the cakes will be soggy. If you are not sure about the oil temperature, flick a drop of water in it. If it pops, it is hot. Pipe batter into pan, and brown both sides. Drain on paper towels. Place on a serving plate, and drizzle syrup over top.

Mary Ann's Banana Bread

Makes 2 loaves plus 1 petite loaf

- 7 large, overripe bananas
- 2 eggs
- 1 1/4 cups sugar
- 1 cup butter
- 1 teaspoon salt, optional
- 2 cups unbleached white flour
- 1 teaspoon baking powder

Preheat oven to 350 degrees F. In a large bowl, combine bananas, eggs, butter, sugar, and salt (if using). Mix by hand between each addition. In a small bowl, combine flour and baking powder. Add to wet ingredients. Mix by hand. Use a pastry cutter, potato masher, or big spoon. Oil and flour two loaf pans as well as one petite loaf pan. Bake large pans 47–48 minutes and petite loaf pan 30 minutes. Test with a toothpick. Remove to cooling rack, and run a knife around the edges of pans. Allow to cool completely before turning out onto waxed paper. Wrap in waxed paper. You may wrap the bread in foil if your family does not gobble it up.

Tips: Allow bananas to ripen between 2 and 4 days. All black is best. Keep overripe bananas in freezer. Thaw prior to using. The key to moist banana bread is nearly fermented, overripe bananas and to have all ingredients at 70 degrees F.

Zucchini Bread

Makes 2 loaves

This bread is moist on the inside and crusty on the outside. You will be pleasantly surprised.

- 3 eggs
- 1 cup canola oil
- 1 cup sugar
- 1 teaspoon vanilla
- 3 cups sifted all-purpose flour
- 2 cups peeled zucchini, grated
- 1 cup chopped walnuts, optional
- 2 teaspoons cinnamon
- 1 teaspoon salt
- 1 teaspoon baking soda
- 1/2 teaspoon baking powder
- 1/2 teaspoon nutmeg

Preheat oven to 325 degrees F. Beat eggs until light and fluffy. Add oil, sugar, and vanilla. Mix well. Add remaining ingredients, and mix well. Butter and flour two large loaf pans, and pour batter in pans. Bake 60 minutes. When a toothpick comes out clean, the bread is ready. Remove to cooling rack for 10 minutes. Turn loaves out of pans on to racks to cool completely.

Dog Food

We love our dogs. When I make dog food, it always has three basic ingredients: beans, rice, and vegetables. Together, this is considered a whole food. I add canola oil for their coats. Sometimes, I have some nice broth that I add. Remember, if it is good for you, it is probably good for them. If it is bad for you, it is probably bad for them. When I cut vegetables or apples, I save the peelings and trimmed vegetable pieces and store them in a gallon zip-top bag in the freezer until it is time to make a batch. With two large dogs, I make large batches and freeze some. You may want to reduce the amounts.

My Basic Dog Food Recipe

Makes about 5 gallons

For the Beans
- 8 cups dried pinto beans, sorted and washed
- canola oil

For the Rice
- canola oil
- 2 zip-top gallon bags frozen vegetable trimmings
- 16 cups water or broth
- 8 cups uncooked rice

For the Beans
In a 12-quart pot, soak beans overnight. You can also use the quick method of bringing to a boil, removing from heat, and letting stand for 1 hour. Drain and rinse. Cover bottom of pot with 1/2-inch canola oil, and return beans to pot. Cover beans with water, and bring to boil. Reduce heat to low, and simmer for 1 hour or until beans are tender.

For the Rice
Cover bottom of 10-quart pot with 1/2-inch canola oil, and cook vegetables until thawed. Add 16 cups water or broth (or a combination) and the rice. Bring to boil, reduce heat to low, and simmer 15 minutes. Remove from heat, and let stand 5 minutes. Combine rice and beans for tasty and healthy dog food.

There are a few foods that dogs need to avoid completely. They are onions, dark chocolate, and most of all, grapes and raisins. There is a lot of information online. My dogs love yams. When I bake them, I always make extra for the dogs. They think they are a treat.

Health Tips

A Little About Health

When I was working, coworkers frequently asked how I stayed in good shape. There are two things: I have always been a swimmer, and I have kept my focus on healthy eating. I learned by experience and self-education that exercise promotes good muscle tone and that a healthy diet promotes weight loss. At one point, I put together a small pamphlet to give out when people asked me how to stay in shape. All the information came from Swedish Hospital and the American Heart Association. I also recommend to anyone that they consult a physician prior to starting any diet or exercise program. I believe that a balanced diet is the only way to go. I enjoy all food groups. It is the portions that are important.

A healthy lifestyle is about choosing the right foods, including fruits, vegetables, whole grains, and unsaturated fats. If you eat more vegetables, you receive two additional benefits. One is that you can eat more. Two is that it takes longer to eat vegetables, so you can spend more time eating. When properly prepared, I find that soups and salads are low in calories and fat and that they can be filling. Among many other websites, you can go to Swedish Hospital in Seattle at www.swedish.org or the American Heart Association website at www.heart.org for recommendations on daily food intake based on a 2,000-calorie diet.

Tips I have learned along the way:

- Take it slow.
- Weigh and measure portions until you have a good feel for amounts.
- Use a salad plate. Prepare your meal, and don't have seconds. If that isn't enough, use a dinner plate, but be sure that at least half of it contains salad and vegetables.
- Read labels.
- Read health articles, and go to health sites online. The more you read on the subject, the better in touch you stay with your goal.
- Weigh yourself frequently.
- Set a top weight that you do not exceed.
- Avoid sauces, dips, and gravy.
- Avoid all-you-can-eat meals like the plague.
- Eat food with fewer calories such as salads and soups. You can have more.
- Wash and prepare vegetables when you get home from the store. You are more likely to eat them if they are ready.
- Prepare food at home. You can make it healthier and delicious.
- Replace salt with herbs and spices.
- If it is a special occasion, treat yourself. Don't let that derail you. Continue your healthy eating.
- Avoid processed food.
- Buy a book with nutritional information, and look up everything you eat.
- Keep a food-and-exercise diary.

I also use small, tempered glass bowls and small bowls from my dishes for portion control. I try to eat a balanced diet and use portion control. I have always based my diet on the Exchange Diet that my doctor gave me years ago. I weighed and measured my food for years. Now I know what my meals should look like. I must admit that since I have retired, I have not been as diligent.

In many of my photos, you'll notice that I have a bowl of tomatoes on my counter. I have tomatoes, two eggs on a bed of spinach, half a pocket bread, and 8 ounces of rice milk most mornings for breakfast. In the summer, I like to keep fresh mint and basil on the counter in a vase. It is easy to use that way.

Index

CPSIA information can be obtained
at www.ICGtesting.com
Printed in the USA
FSOW03n2340230817
37869FS